About the editors

Bill and Marta Annett together run a small consultancy in London. Bill served in the Royal Artillery during the 1939–45 war, after which he spent twenty five years in advertising and public relations, before setting up the present partnership.

Marta is Hungarian, born and brought up in Budapest during the difficult years of the thirties and forties and provides the logic, judgment and critical ability essential to a man-and-wife operation.

The compilation of *Winning Through* is an expression of gratitude for a very happy partnership, both in marriage and in business – their own 'winning through' from some of Life's knocks – and the recognition of the way in which their own two sons have grown up to justify their faith in them.

*Not in the clamour of the crowded street,
Not in the shouts and plaudits of the throng,
But in ourselves, are triumph and defeat.*

          Longfellow

WINNING THROUGH

How People Have Triumphed Over Tragedy

Foreword by George Thomas,
Viscount Tonypandy

Edited by Bill and Marta Annett

CENTURY
LONDON MELBOURNE AUCKLAND JOHANNESBURG

Grateful acknowledgement is made for permission to quote from the following works:

What This Katie Did by Katie Boyle, published by Weidenfeld (Publishers) Limited; *Our Kate* by Catherine Cookson, by permission of Anthony Sheil Associates Ltd; *Dennis Flanders' Britannia* by Dennis Flanders, published by Oriel Press, now Routledge & Kegan Paul.

Copyright © The Contributors 1987
Introduction © Bill and Marta Annett 1987

All rights reserved

First published in 1987 by Century Hutchinson Ltd,
62–65 Chandos Place, London, WC2N 4NW

Century Hutchinson Australia Pty Ltd,
PO Box 496, 16–22 Church Street, Hawthorn, Victoria 3122, Australia

Century Hutchinson New Zealand Limited,
PO Box 40–086, Glenfield, Auckland 10, New Zealand

Century Hutchinson South Africa (Pty) Ltd,
PO Box 337, Bergvlei 2012, South Africa

Typset by Avocet Marketing Services, Bicester, Oxon.

Printed and bound in Great Britain by
Richard Clay Ltd, Bungay, Suffolk

British Library Cataloguing in Publication Data

Winning through : how people have
triumphed over tragedy.
1. Conduct of life 2. Life skills
3. Problem solving
I. Annett, Bill II. Annett, Marta
158'.1   BF637.C5

ISBN 0-7126-1600-4

Contents

Editors' Introduction — vii
Foreword by Viscount Tonypandy — ix
The National Children's Home — xi

Contributors
The Duchess of Bedford	1
Humphry Berkeley	5
Sheila Black OBE	9
The Most Rev. and Rt. Hon. Lord Blanch DD LLD MA	13
Katie Boyle	16
John Bratby RA ARCA RBA FIAL FRSA	19
Julia Clements VMH	22
Catherine Cookson OBE MA	26
Baroness Cox	30
Constance Cummings CBE	34
Robin Day OBE RDI ARCA FSIAD	36
Shirley Anne Field	40
Dennis Flanders RWS RBA	44
Christina Foyle	48
The Rt. Rev. The Bishop of Gibraltar in Europe	51
Beryl Grey CBE D Mus D Litt	55
Sir Charles Groves CBE FRCM	58
General Sir John Hackett GCB CBE DSO MC	61
Illtyd Harrington JP	64
Rachael Heyhoe Flint MBE	69
Sir Immanuel Jakobovits the Chief Rabbi	73

Miriam Karlin	76
Colonel Ronald Kaulback OBE	80
Esmond Knight	84
Peter Macann	88
Robert Maxwell MC	92
Stirling Moss OBE	95
Countess Mountbatten of Burma CD JP DL	98
The Very Rev. I. D. Neill CB OBE	102
Juliet Pannett FRSA	106
David Shepherd OBE FRSA	110
Dinah Sheridan	114
Rosemary Anne Sisson	117
Wayne Sleep	121
The Rev. The Lord Soper MA PhD	124
Wing Cmdr. R. Stanford-Tuck DSO DFC (2 bars)	128
Dr Miriam Stoppard MD MRCP	133
Lance Thirkell	135
Wendy Toye	139
Nigel Tranter OBE	142
Baroness Trumpington	145
Ravenna Tucker	149
Charles Vance	153
Ian Wallace OBE	158
Sidney Weighell	162
Air Chief Marshal Sir Neil Wheeler GCB CBE DSO DFC AFC	166
Laurence Whistler CBE FRSL	170
Phillip Whitehead	173
Mary Whitehouse CBE	178

Introduction

Tragedy, misfortune and personal crisis are part of the pattern of everyday life. They strike a balance with happiness, achievement and good fortune, but human nature renders them more newsworthy, as a study of the media will confirm.

He, or she, who goes through life without trouble is a rarity, but when Fate strikes the individual, the victim tends to ask, 'why me?' and to look around at all the world carrying on happily and quite unaffected, even if superficially sympathetic.

Self-pity is negative and destructive and to push it to one side is essential if tragedies, misfortunes and crises are to be overcome and survived. It is commonly assumed that those who enjoy public acclaim inhabit a higher plane than the average person in the street, immune from sorrow or the kind of worry which visits the rest of us. We therefore thought it would be in the general interest to dispel this misapprehension and to seek the collaboration of some of those in the public eye whom Life has not always treated fairly; people who have shared the kind of crises known to so many of us and who have overcome, or come to terms with them by determination, optimism and faith. We set out on this journey in all innocence, oblivious of the difficulties. Why should people of note agree to reveal personal experiences, in many cases of a harrowing nature, for others to read in cold print? Why should we think that the kind of people we had in mind, would have time to compose a chapter of 750 to 1,000 words on a delicate subject? And did we not know that all famous people are bombarded daily with requests to write for charity books? A cool, clear mind might, at the first suggestion of the venture, have advised against starting it at all. However, we were encouraged by the support of the National Children's Home, to whom the royalties are to be donated, and of Century Hutchinson Ltd., who assessed the feasibility and agreed to publish the book provided we could enlist the cooperation of the required number of well-known contributors.

The next step was to make our approaches to famous people, all but a few unknown to us personally. This has been a most rewarding and enjoyable experience, through which we have met many interesting people and made a number of new friends, even among those who, for one reason or another, felt unable to become involved. We would like to thank all those who have written for the book and in addition those kind people who, in lieu of writing, sent a donation for the charity.

The seal is set upon the book by the Viscount Tonypandy who, in his capacity as Chairman of the National Children's Home, has written the foreword. We are very grateful to him for his cooperation.

We hope that all who read *Winning Through* will take heart from the experiences related and that the book will bring encouragement, hope and joy to those who are striving to overcome their own crises.

BILL AND MARTA ANNETT

Foreword

Reading through the list of distinguished contributors to this book is to catch a glimpse of people who have enriched the life of our country in so many ways: in the arts, in the pulpit, in the debating chambers of politics, on the battlefields, in literature, and through sheer adventure.

Like most other people they have faced setbacks at sometime in their lives which threatened to block the potential that finally led them to success.

I faced trauma in my early years in Wales and in the difficult times in my life as a politician. But my Christian faith and the support of my mother, family and friends were an unfailing source of strength for me.

I am particularly grateful to the authors of this book for donating the proceeds to the National Children's Home, of which I am Chairman. The work of the NCH, like all charities, has changed since its inception. The ways in which the needs of the deprived and of the damaged are met have altered but unhappily there is no change in the need for the help we provide.

The NCH has found some success with its Children in Danger Campaign which seeks to protect growing numbers of children who are exposed to tragic dangers of abduction, of sexual abuse, of violence and of drugs, as well as of the seemingly ever present problems of poverty, homelessness and the breakdown of family life.

I have been particularly concerned with the Missing Link

Project that aims to establish contact with the depressingly large and ever increasing number of children who run away from home to London and other large cities where they are exposed to dangers that can destroy them.

Thanks to God, and to the devoted caring staff of the NCH there are success stories to go alongside the tragic. Among my most pleasurable duties as chairman of the NCH are my visits to the Homes which invariably ring with the unique sound of happy laughter and chatter that comes only from contented children playing together.

As you read through these pages you will each be struck by one particular moment that will stay with you long after you put the book down. For me, perhaps the most heartening story is that of Shirley Anne Field, the gifted actress, who was sent to the National Children's Home as a small child. It was there that she learnt the values and strength of spirit that helped her through her adult years.

Here is a success story for the NCH. Your support in buying this book helps to ensure that our work continues to meet the changing needs of children who, for whatever reason, are deprived of the normal happy home life which the rest of us take for granted.

Thank you for your support, thanks to all who contributed to this book, may God Bless you and the children and our every endeavour in the NCH.

Tonypandy   Cardiff, January 1987

The National Children's Home

There have been two periods of great activity in the 118-year life of the National Children's Home. The first 20 years under its founder, the Rev Thomas Stephenson, saw tremendous innovation with the coining of a new concept in child care – a children's home, not a workhouse or a ragged school but a place of warmth and caring. Within a few years, homes were set up in rural and urban England, a protective emigration system to Canada was established, a home for children with special needs, and the first of the industrial schools, following legislation to clear the streets of vagrant juveniles, were founded. NCH bristled with active concern.

Since NCH's centenary in 1969, the organisation has changed radically whilst remaining true to its founding spirit. Gradually the large children's homes have given way to small residential units for children, able and disabled, with special needs. A number of special schools provide comprehensive care for youngsters with a variety of handicaps – physical, mental, educational, emotional; and most have now developed extended education units for children above school-leaving age but who could still profit from fulfilling their potential for independent living. Many independence preparation units now also exist for care leavers with no suitable home to return to.

The main thrust of modern development is in the field of family support. In community projects and family centres (for families referred by local authorities) support is given to (mostly) lone-parent families suffering from poverty, bad housing and usually an inability to cope. The success and cost effectiveness of these centres is so apparent, it is clear that a greater number of these spread throughout urban Britain would be a major step forward in preventing neglect and ill treatment. A nationwide phone-in service, NCH Careline, manned by trained volunteers round the clock, receives thousands of calls from young people in distress or despair over the problems they are facing in their family or private life.

Another major area of NCH development is in the field of juvenile justice. Too many young people receive custodial treatment for crimes that do not warrant it. NCH offers day and weekend treatment for young offenders called Intermediate Treatment which works positively on the challenges in a young person's life. The success rate is far greater than that of Borstals and detention centres, and magistrates are beginning to refer more and more young people to IT.

NCH has launched a Children in Danger Campaign of public awareness and private lobbying. It produces an annual update of official child-related statistics and sees itself as a voice for all children in need. NCH's strength is that every word it utters for children is based on its daily care and support of the neediest people in society today.

NCH now cares for over 9,000 children and families in over 140 centres in the United Kingdom.

John F. Gray
Director of Advocacy
National Children's Home

The Duchess of Bedford

The Duchess of Bedford was born in France, the daughter of Paul Schneider, the celebrated French air ace of the First World War, and worked for the Resistance during the 1939-45 war.

Married to the Duke of Bedford in 1960, she now lives in Monaco. The Duchess has four children by a previous marriage.

I was born in France, so during the war and the period when France was occupied by the Germans, a friend from my youth asked me to be a courier for the Resistance. I agreed. As he kindly said, 'I looked so naive and stupid, I would make a good, inconspicuous one.' I was then twenty-three, but never having worn make-up and having long hair to the bottom of my back, I indeed looked very innocent.

Petrol was an unknown commodity for the French, being only used by the Germans and for factory work. The French population went about either by the metro, or on foot, but mostly by bicycle. I was the proud owner of a white and green bicycle, which had striped canvas saddlebags of the same colours over the back wheel. I would receive cryptic messages, such as, 'the rose has bloomed,' or, 'the babies are born,' which in code meant I had to go to a certain address where I would receive a parcel in old newspapers, put it in the bag on my bicycle, pedal through Paris, pass the German gendarmes, and go to a given address to deliver it. I soon learned to recognize by touch money, machine-guns in pieces, etc. This went on for months until 15 July, 1944 when part of our group had returned, bicycling late after their deliveries. One of the girls who did not see a post, bumped into it with her bicycle. The front wheel was twisted and her knee gashed.

The group was transporting equipment for making identity cards and passports. They started walking in the night and were eventually stopped by the German curfew patrol, the 'green,' as we called them. One of the boys who spoke German went ahead and distracted the two soldiers, while another one at the back of the group chose a building which had a double door for car entry knowing that, at this time in Paris, there was an automatic release catch and he could get rid of the equipment behind the front door, which he did. The group was taken as usual to the police station and had to perform tasks such as cleaning windows and floors, or polishing boots, etc.

At 5 a.m. at daybreak they were released, and the word among them passed to meet at mid-day in the regular meeting point which was an attic in Neuilly, a residential suburb of Paris, to tell everyone in the group to disband, preferably to the country and not to return to their usual address.

I received the message. It was a very hot day. The message did not explain that there was any danger, only that we would meet for fifteen minutes. As I arrived, I remembered that the heat in the attic would be unbearable and as there was no water in the attic, I went to a fruit stand and bought two pounds of black cherries, so as fate had it I was five minutes late for the meeting. When I arrived at the address, I could see the black limousine in front of the building. In France, black limousines during occupation time meant only one thing, GESTAPO. So I stood there, planted on the pavement, paralyzed, looking at the front door of the building. One by one all my friends came out, manacled and at gunpoint, being pushed into the waiting cars. They could all see me standing, looking at them in my gay summer clothes holding my bags of cherries, fear and panic registering in their eyes. A little girl passing will never understand why she was given cherries. I started walking, thinking hard and fast where to find help.

Once out of view, I jumped on my bicycle and started to pedal furiously to tell all the parents of my friends what was happening. As it was the middle of the summer I found practically no one. The ones I found were terrified... 'have you been followed?'... 'will they recognize you?'... etc.

All the group were taken to a concentration camp in Germany, including the man who owned the attic who was not even part of the group. Out of eighteen people, he was the only one who returned.

I started my desperate search for help. I went to the Kommandanture, the German High Command Post, and all of the places I could think of to try to locate the place where they had been taken, but to no avail. The end of the war was very close, a month, and the Germans were in total panic.

Despair engulfed me.

One morning when I was in my Faubourg St Honoré apartment, the doorbell rang and a very large lady wearing the typical black pleated skirt of the market people was at the door. She explained that she saw the trucks going to Germany, full of young people. Her son was a prisoner of war; one of my friends' eyes met hers, he had dropped his arm outside of the truck and dropped a little note, folded and folded again to the size of a thumbnail. It had my name and address on it. The little note was a cry for help and I felt even more hopeless with it. I went to see the mother of the young man and we tried again all of the various things including the Red Cross, with absolutely no success, no news, and a demented hopeless feeling looking at the map of Germany knowing they were somewhere, but where?

A friend of mine whom I visited regularly to read or to chat to, as he had polio and was in an iron lung, saw my puffy red eyes and knew of the situation, and he said, 'the sun is shining, the flowers are blooming, you can walk freely, so you should be grateful.' At that point I was reading to him a poem full of hope and joy. I decided that despair was not constructive and self-pity even less so, and I forced myself to snap out of it.

The war ended on 26 August. Paris was liberated. The brother of the boy who had sent me the note appeared in a jeep with General Leclerc. He was in a victorious mood and I had to tell him the sad tale of our group, but his enthusiasm was not dampened for a minute. He said, 'I will go and deliver them, trust me.' In fact, General Leclerc and his division went on fighting and advancing to the east of France. His ADC, my friend, dashingly went to plant the French national flag on the Strasbourg Cathedral spire and was shot by a rooftop sniper! But his enthusiasm had been passed to me.

Every day I would go to Hotel Lutece where the prisoners returned from concentration camps. I waited, and waited, and waited every day and watched those atrociously emaciated people in their striped pyjamas. Finally, one day the man who lent us the attic appeared. He told me that all of our friends were dead, but he survived despite a stomach ulcer, which was cured by eating sawdust bread, staple diet of concentration camps. He said he was saved because being an artist he drew when he could on anything with everything, charcoal, twig, etc. and that way had saved his sanity. At night when he was hungry and frozen he would try to memorize all of the symphonies and concertos that he knew. And that saved him.

As I wrote in my book, *Nicole Nobody*, blind hope is a delusion and a weakness. When hardship comes, *Aides toi, le Ciel t'aidera.*' Help yourself and God will help you.

Humphry Berkeley

Humphry Berkeley was born in 1926, the son of the playwright Reginald Berkeley. He was educated at the Dragon School, Oxford, and Pembroke College, Cambridge, where he became President of the Union and Chairman of the Cambridge University Conservative Association.

From 1959-66 he was MP for Lancaster and from 1961-65 he was a Member of the Council of Europe at Strasbourg and of the Council of Western European Union in Paris.

From 1966-70 he chaired the United Nations Association of Great Britain and Northern Ireland and during the same period was a member of the UK National Commission for UNESCO and a member of Prince Philip's Committee on Overseas Volunteers.

Humphry Berkeley is a broadcaster and the author of a number of books with a political background. He is now the SDP/Liberal Alliance candidate for Southend East and is also the director of a leukaemia charity.

The manner of his survival from the terrifying experience he relates below can only be described as a miracle.

~~~~~~~~~~~~~~~~~~~~~~

It happened on the night of Thursday 15 February 1979. I was having dinner, alone, in the Holiday Inn, Umtata, the capital of Transkei, the first homeland to be granted independence by South Africa, and the only one that could genuinely qualify for independent statehood. It is a geographical whole, has a coastline of two hundred miles, a population of two million, and had, with virtually identical borders, been ceded to Queen Victoria in 1879. I was seeking to get it international recognition.

I was told during dinner that two people were waiting to see me. I sent for one of them who told me that he was a member of the Transkei Security Police. Despite the fact that I had been working for the Prime Minister of Transkei, Chief Kaiser Matanzima, for nearly a year, I sensed that something unusual was about to happen and I was determined to remain calm. 'I do not see people without prior appointment,' I said severely, 'You will have to wait in the reception area for about half an hour.' As there were many other people dining in the restaurant I assumed, correctly, that I would not be removed by force.

When I went into the reception area I was handed a warrant for my arrest for fraud. Although the document appeared to be authentic the charge was absurd. The only money which came to me was a quarterly fee for my services. All journeys overseas, of which there were many, had to receive the prior authorization of the Prime Minister and all expenses were scrutinized and approved by him, personally. I refused to go to the police station. I was suddenly seized by them, bundled out of the hotel and told to get into a car. I refused to do so until they had picked up the contents of my briefcase, which they did.

As we drove down the hotel drive another car moved in behind us. I was driven slowly to a remote spot about five miles outside Umtata. I was ordered to get out of the car by the two Security Police Officers and four other Africans got out of the car behind. The six men then proceeded to beat me up. Five of them appeared to have whips but one of them must have had a belt with a metal buckle as the injuries to my head subsequently made clear. I was knocked to the ground several times and once I became unconscious for several seconds after a blow on my head.

'Why don't you kill me?' I shouted, 'We are going to do so,' replied one of my assailants, 'but we will do so in our own way.' I had lost all sense of time as blows kept thudding on my body and head. Eventually the beating stopped. My hands and feet were tied together with rough pieces of rope. I was lifted into the boot of the Datsun car in which I had been driven to the place of my assault. The boot was slammed shut and the car was driven away.

My first sensation was one of relief. The blows which had rained down upon my body had stopped. I ached everywhere. Slowly I regained my composure. While I cannot claim to have lived a very virtuous life, I have always been the fortunate recipient of religious faith. For many years I have said my prayers daily, and have attended Mass and received Communion every Sunday. I have never said a prayer that has gone unanswered. It did not occur to me to pray that my life might be spared; rather, I prayed that God would give me the strength to endure whatever lay ahead. Before long I was calm and totally without fear, and in mental tranquility I awaited the end.

After we had driven for about two hours the car paused and I heard the driver say, 'police'. At last I understood the plan. We had crossed the border into South Africa. I was to be shot dead and my body would be found on the side of a road in South Africa where I was a prohibited person.

Shortly afterwards the car came to a halt, in what I was later to discover was a deserted side road. I was taken out of the boot and was so weak that I could hardly stand. Three Africans faced me. The middle and tallest of them pointed a revolver at me and said, 'Now I am going to shoot you.' I heard myself say, 'I am not afraid of being killed but it is very wicked to kill an innocent man. Kneel down and I will ask God to forgive you for what you are about to do.' My three captors fell to their knees and I made the sign of the cross over each of them saying, 'May God forgive you.' After this they jumped to their feet, got into their car and drove away.

Two or three minutes later a car passed me and I managed to flag it down. I asked to be taken to the nearest police station which turned out to be in a small village called Komga. The officer in charge drove me to a hospital less than a quarter of a mile away. A night sister was on duty. I saw that my face and hair were covered in blood. A surgeon arrived and put eight stitches into my head and gave me a massive blood transfusion. The hospital records show that I was expected to die within twelve hours.

It was the most extraordinary experience of my life. I had escaped death three times, first when my captors fled, secondly when a car miraculously came down a deserted road and thirdly when, against all expectations, I survived the surgery and loss of blood.

The warrant for my arrest, which a magistrate told me he had seen, disappeared. My docket in the Transkei Ministry of Police also disappeared. I returned to Transkei, against the advice of my friends, to confront the Prime Minister and identify the culprits. They were never punished and the South African Government, despite the intervention of the British Foreign Secretary, refused to extradite them. I shall always wonder why God gave me such strength. I did not ask for it, but it was given in abundance. Even now, after nine years, I dare not question His purpose.

Sheila Black OBE

Born in Sri Lanka on Buddha's birthday and christened Sheila Psyche Black, she always wanted to be called by her middle name, but 'nobody ever took to it.' Educated in Dorset and Switzerland, she joined RADA and became an actress, but her theatrical career was cut short by marriage, war and motherhood, in that order.

Postwar, firstly in advertising, she found her métier in journalism in the mid-fifties. She was Woman's Editor of the *Financial Times* from 1959 to 1972 and a features writer for many newspapers and magazines. Chairman of the new Gas Consumers' Council (as she was of its predecessor), she is also a member of the National Consumer Council and the Council of the Institute of Directors.

Sheila Black still writes periodically and lists her recreations as horticulture in London, grandchildren and football.

She was awarded an OBE in 1986.

∞∞∞∞∞∞∞∞∞∞∞∞∞∞∞

'You'll probably never get out of a wheelchair. You'll certainly never walk again without crutches.'

The doctor said it kindly enough, but with matter-of-irrefutable-fact conviction. Since the paralysis was, and had been, total for a few weeks, there was no reason to doubt him and other specialists who had called to check up on me.

It was evening. And May, a few days from my twenty-ninth birthday. Clearly, life was over, had nothing more to offer.

Through the dark night I puzzled about how to kill myself in a busy hospital with no use of either hands or feet.

In the morning, it snowed. After strong, warm April sunshine the snow came down softly, gently and lay on the ground, its untrampled whiteness reminding me of how my children and I had muddied the winter snow as we fought our snowball battles.

The children. Good heavens, I had been so full of my own self-pity that I had totally forgotten them and how I loved them, how I would miss them. Of course, I couldn't exactly miss them if I were dead, but how terrible it would be to miss their growing-up, their developing lives. Of course, I had to live. NO. Of course, I wanted to live. Really wanted to. But how?

I was then on the threshold of a career in advertising, one that would be difficult to pursue from a wheelchair, with no useful hands...

'Why not try writing?' suggested the doctor. 'You can do it a little. You may not be able to hold a pen but I'm sure you could tackle a typewriter!' And, bless his Scottish heart, he arranged to borrow one for me and have it set up on a bed-table, removing me to a corner of the ward so as not to disturb others.

He had been right. I could punch the keys, even if I couldn't feel them. I didn't achieve very accurate results but readable enough if I went slowly and laboriously. I had trouble when it came to making inked corrections legibly and neatly but kind friends were more than helpful.

I was still in hospital when my first article, the first I wrote, was accepted. By a trade paper, yes, a booksellers' paper. But acceptance and a cheque for ten pounds were the Oscar for my efforts, the incentives to do it again.

It was some time before I actually got anyone to hire me as a writer, though freelance articles were often accepted. My former employers were wonderful when I went back to them but I wanted to write for a living, not as a sideline. They treated me rather as an invalid, cosseting me instead of accepting me as whole. They meant well.

I became successful and well-known, if that doesn't sound too immodest. On the *Financial Times*, I had a wonderful time. I travelled the world, learned much about many industries and people, and lived a full, varied life.

And I loved it, enjoyed it all so much. My grandchildren, too, were – indeed are – sources of deep pleasure and I occasionally shudder to think I had ever wanted anything but to live. What I would have missed. Oh yes, I would have missed tragedy and heartache and pain too. But I would also have missed learning how much life has to be a blend of happiness and sadness. The old adage cannot be gainsaid. 'The brighter the sunshine, the deeper the shadow.' But think about that. The reverse is true, isn't it?

The difference is in accepting that other side of the coin. When, in my extreme youth, I had been an actress, we would peer between the closed curtains of the theatre at the audience and sigh. 'The house is half empty,' we would wail. But, to the box office manager, it was half full.

That is the point. Looking on the positive side, believing that the house is half full, that the lights will go up again, knowing that the darker the scene, the brighter those lights will be. Whatever has happened has taught me the joy and power of survival. The ability to accept the unacceptable and unpredictable, to live with change. Well... to live.

I learned gratitude for life itself. I learned deep appreciation, with sharpened senses, of sad and happy, beautiful and ugly, positive and negative. And that you never have as much time as you think.

The paralysis? Oh, I was very lucky. I did learn to walk and was lucky enough to be physically active again. The crisis, for me, was not being paralyzed. It was neither moral nor mental, except in the sense that every crisis is one, the other or both. The crisis was facing sudden deprivation, trying to make the impossible just possible.

Like most people, I had a stalwart to support me. I never actually liked that doctor. He had no bedside manner and he was pretty hard, almost ruthless and heartless in his bluntness, his determination to tell the worst possible truths.

He never gave me hope. But he gave me courage. He gave me time. He gave me resentment, anger, resistance, bloody-mindedness, all the weapons I needed at a time when I had none. Oh, and he gave me that typewriter.

He also gave me a career I would never have chased otherwise. A life that I would never have been able to live.

A fulfilment.

The Most Rev. & Rt. Hon. Lord Blanch DD LLD MA

Lord Blanch was Archbishop of York from 1975–83. Born in 1918 in the Forest of Dean and educated at Alleyns School, Dulwich, he spent four years in insurance before serving as a navigator in the RAF from 1940–46. After the war he read theology at Wycliffe Hall, Oxford (BA 1st Class 1948, MA 1952) and after five years as Vicar of Eynsham he returned to Wycliffe Hall as Vice Principal until 1960. Oriel Canon of Rochester and Warden of Rochester Theological College for the next six years, he became Bishop of Liverpool until 1975 when he was enthroned as Archbishop of York. Honoured with a Life Peerage in 1983, Lord Blanch is Pro-Chancellor of the Universities of Hull and of York, Sub-Prelate of the Order of St John and has Hon. Doctorates of four universities. He has also written eight books on aspects of religious faith.

Lord Blanch is married and has one son and four daughters.

∞∞∞∞∞∞∞∞∞∞∞∞

There are certain stress situations to which every human being is subject and which are only too familiar to the medical profession – the new school, the first job, marriage, the arrival of a family, a serious illness, bereavement, retirement. In the case of my generation, add to the list the experience of call-up, and those grim early days in the services. But there is one stress situation which, so it seems, particularly affects those who are constantly in the public eye. The experienced actor suddenly succumbs to stage-fright. The accomplished speaker finds himself for no apparent reason speechless. The seasoned politician without any warning loses all zest for the battle. The busy clergyman moving confidently amongst difficult but familiar things awakens to the sense of painful emptiness and inadequacy within himself.

I was Bishop and subsequently Archbishop for nearly twenty years, enjoying on the whole remarkably good health, tested but also sustained by the responsibilities of public office. It was a busy life, of long days and incessant travel, with much speaking and much writing, with awkward decisions to make and unfamiliar situations to face. I did not suffer from doubts about my vocation or about my capacity to fulfil it – after a fashion. And then suddenly after Christmas one year I was assailed with an unaccountable sense of malaise and a feeling of incapacity for even the most modest demands which were made upon me. The immediate crisis was soon over – a month free from public engagements and a short holiday in the sun, the occasional evening at home and a slightly more leisurely start to each day.

The crisis was short, the consequences more far-reaching. For I had to accept that I was not, as I had fondly imagined, invulnerable to stress, that I could not always be confidently in charge of my own life, that, in short, I was a mortal man, no longer immune to the accidents of time and circumstance. It was no more than a symptom, but a sympton can be a very alarming thing; it can change a man's view of life, challenge his estimate of himself and provoke a drastic change of outlook on the world and on eternity. The short holiday in the sun was one thing, the long 'convalescence' was quite another thing. There was no way I could just laugh it off or find relief in renewed activity. I had to ask myself where I really stood in relation to my job and in relation to my God. But then this is what faith is all about – not just health and high spirits or assent to certain doctrines but the discovery by a needy man about his need for the indispensable resources of God. During this period of reduced activity I turned over and over again to a book I had not read for years – *Abandonment to Divine Providence* by De Caussade. 'Abandonment', in his vocabulary, is just another word for faith, it meant recognizing my own folly and fallibility, coming to terms with my mortality and abandoning myself to one who is at the same time infinitely remote in the heavens and preciously near to anyone who is of a humble and contrite spirit.

I did not enjoy the symptoms; it meant some sleepless nights and undue anxieties about the next engagement; it left me sometimes with a chronic lassitude and a recurring depression. I was fortunate in having a firm but understanding doctor, a loving family and a supportive staff. But even with all these human assets I would scarcely have survived without the faith which I had discovered during my days in the RAF or without the steady conviction born of a patient study of the Scriptures which enabled me to affirm, if I did not always feel, that I was in the hand of One who loved me and had a purpose for my life beyond my immediate perceptions of it. I can now say with St Paul, and mean it, that 'The outward man does indeed suffer wear and tear, but every day the inward man receives fresh strength. These little troubles (which are really so transitory) are winning for us a permanent, glorious and solid reward out of all proportion to our pain.' (2 Corinthians 4, 16, 17 – J. B. Phillips' translation)

In my case it was not so much a matter of winning through, but of holding on.

Katie Boyle

Famous as a TV and radio personality, former international fashion model and, for the past sixteen years 'Dear Katie' in the *TV Times Magazine* – Katie Boyle is the daughter of an Italo-Russian nobleman and an Anglo-Australian mother.

A traumatic childhood, and an expensive, but chequered, education was the prelude to a life of greatly varied experience and mixed fortunes. In this excerpt from her autobiography *What This Katie Did*, she describes the loss of a beloved husband after many years of happy marriage – and how she came to terms with widowhood.

∞∞∞∞∞∞∞∞∞∞∞∞∞∞∞

The telephone rang. Short, persistent rings nagged me out of the deepest sleep. I looked at my little clock. It glowed 4.30 a.m. Where was I? I couldn't remember. The bell shrilled again. There must be some mistake. I groped vaguely towards the bell – I couldn't find the light.

'Yes,' I growled.

'Is that Miss Boyle?' I'd never heard the voice before.

'Yes,' I snapped, impatiently this time.

'I have some bad news for you – your husband is dead!'

I remember nothing. Teresa, our housekeeper, who was standing next to that heartless doctor, says my screams through the telephone were blood-curdling.

Greville was killed by a massive coronary thrombosis – that scourge as endemic to this age as smallpox was to the 14th century. It's a bitter indictment against this age too that I was immediately offered pills to dull my despair. I refused them all, for to camouflage my emotions, even on the day of his funeral, I felt would be unworthy of Greville, as well as make it worse for me later.

Then, four days after the funeral, I decided I had to honour my contract with Woolworth's. Nine whole weeks of a show in a different town every single night, except for Sundays. The effort of travelling non-stop to all the places, as well as visiting Girlie (the small bitch we had brought back from a Kenyan beach) in the quarantine kennels, drained all the physical energy from me. What carried me through emotionally was the warmth of the audiences. Each one seemed to consist of individuals who felt my anguish and willed me to get through the show. The models were also towers of strength. In fact, to everyone involved in that painful marathon I shall always be eternally grateful. Looking back on it all now, perhaps it even saved my sanity.

My work was so pressurised for weeks on end that only several months after Greville's death did I begin to realize just how much loneliness, how much vulnerability, is welded into that word 'widow'. The difference between organizing and getting on with everyday details when Greville was in the background was enormous in comparison to coping alone. But it was a relief and a comfort to telephone Teresa every night and morning and go back home to her on Sundays. She, as well as Joan – my daily who has been with me for twenty-eight years – were closely involved in our highs and lows. Now they were determined to do all they could, despite their own shock and grief, to help me.

It may seem odd, but from the very first moments, when the smithereens of my world threatened to submerge me, I was aware of the importance of words. To begin with there were the letters. They poured in. I would never have believed they could have been of such comfort. But they were. Whether they came from friends, acquaintances or strangers, their warmth, the knowledge that people cared enough to write, was incredibly reassuring.

All those words I read over and over again, and took comfort from them when I needed it so badly. But I think the ones which helped me most to survive instant widowhood are these, written by Canon Scott Holland, who was an eminent theologian during Queen Victoria's reign. I believe them implicitly:

Death is nothing at all – I have only slipped away into the next room. I am I, and you are you. Whatever we were to each other, that we still are. Call me by my old familiar name, speak to me in the easy way which you always used. Wear no forced air of solemnity or sorrow. Laugh as we always laughed at the little jokes we enjoyed together. Play, smile, think of me, pray for me. Let my name be ever the household word that it always was. Let it be spoken without effect, without the ghost of a shadow on it. Life means all that it ever meant. It is the same as it ever was. There is absolutely unbroken continuity. What is this death but a negligible accident? Why should I be out of mind because I am out of sight? I am waiting for you – for an interval – somewhere very near just around the corner. All is well.

I am convinced of that continuity of life to life through death – and I am equally certain that the bridge between the two worlds is built on Love. I know that I am laughed at for my beliefs but I don't mind and I feel it isn't up to me to try and change people's minds on this subject. I'm just sure that so many things have happened to me, and their repetition goes way beyond coincidence. After all why should anyone be so conceited as to feel that we are the ultimate in knowledge and experience?

One thing is for sure: without my beliefs I would never have had the resilience to bounce back from some of the body blows life has dealt me.

John Bratby RA ARCA RBA FIAL FRSA

One of Britain's foremost contemporary painters, John Bratby has exhibited at the Royal Academy regularly for the past thirty years, has held numerous one-man exhibitions here and abroad and has also shown pictures in various international exhibitions and festivals. He has also found time to write a number of books, a TV play and to contribute illustrations to the Oxford Illustrated Old Testament. He acts as Editorial Adviser to Art Quarterly. His contribution to this book is as colourful and vital as his paintings.

∞∞∞∞∞∞∞∞∞∞∞∞∞∞

In a colourful life of 58 years, the hardest period, without doubt, was the male menopause, a condition that, contrary to some scepticism, does exist as a reality and not only as a joke made up by comedians.

Many terrible things happened to me in that period when I was a lost being. The time was at the end of 1972 and in 1973. In the middle of a divorce, between the *decree nisi* and a *decree absolute*, I suffered an aggressive hiatus, when financial settlement was overshadowed by the fury of a long marriage ended.

I had two spectacular car crashes. The first one, while racing to meet my new girlfriend, wrote off my white Mercedes, leaving me to meet her with blood on my forehead.

But the second was the more serious. I had bought a beautiful new Mercedes 230SL, red, and one evening, in London, I drove it out of a multi-storey car park and picked up my girlfriend in the street below after a courteous black attendant had bid me good-night.

She told me she wanted to go home and not to stay in the handsome flat I had rented as a love nest, and that she was going abroad to Portugal. I was devastated. She was all I had ever wanted and now I had virtually lost her. I remembered how she had left our apartment near Brighton after a beautiful time together. Now I felt betrayed and rejected.

I am happy now, but then I felt she and she alone was my only chance of sunshine – an opportunity to compensate for a disappointing youth. By the time I met her I seemed to have achieved everything, was jaded and life's future was nothing to look forward to – just seeing the children into art school or university and feeling more and more middle-aged in comparison with their competitive youth. We had lived together and I was besotted. She was in her mid-twenties and to me a goddess. All the dullness of the last years of my first marriage acted as a foil to the glitter of the new relationship.

During the relationship I painted her scores of times – showed them at the Royal Academy – had whole one-man exhibitions – they were love paintings and they all sold, I thought, because my passion was infectious and was transmitted.

When I realized I was losing her I cried and raged like a child whose favourite toy is snatched away and suffered more than I had ever done before or since. What point was there in living? I was losing my jewel. In the torment of deprivation I pushed the accelerator down to the floor and the powerful and beautiful car shot forward at top speed. A car ahead of me stopped at traffic lights and the red Mercedes I was driving crashed into the back. I imagined I was driving to oblivion into a wall. My head drove into the windscreen which was so made that it did not break but moulded to my head. I have photographs that show the gaping bonnet – lid pointing skywards and the shape of my skull in the windscreen. Blood poured down my face. 'My love, my love', cried my melodramatic sweetheart, holding my head in her hands.

Later I chased her in aeroplanes to Portugal. Casanova may have exaggerated his escape through the leads of the roof of the Doge's Palace, but my account is factual. I mourned my love for a long time but in retrospect I can see how pathetic, childish and silly I had been. Still thinking of her I wrote in reply to an advertisement in *Time Out*. The lady I met I did not love at first but I married her and went on honeymoon to Paris where, in the Rue de Rivoli next day, I found all the English papers full of photographs and chat about our marriage. That was nine years ago.

The marriage was stormy for years. We had both had a rough time, were savaged people and not gentle as a result, but in the last few years we have found that we love each other and life for us both is rich and as I have never known it before. I must have a thousand colour photographs of her stuck to the walls of the rooms of the vast and beautiful white house in which we live by the sea. It may sound corny but I have found happiness at last. Of course it's not perfect, but it's a damn good deal of the cards.

Julia Clements VMH

Author, speaker, teacher and international judge of floral art, Julia Clements is the widow of the late Sir Alexander Hay Seton Bt. A pioneer in the expressive art of flower arranging for the masses after the 1939–45 war, she helped form clubs and organized the first judges' school at the Royal Horticultural Society's Halls in London. She does not professionally decorate, nor has she a shop or business, but travels the world teaching, demonstrating and lecturing to all those who need her. She was awarded the Victoria Medal of Honour by the Royal Horticultural Society for her pioneer work in forming Flower Clubs and she has the unique distinction of having three roses named after her: Julia Clements, Lady Seton and Julia's Rose. She has twenty books on the subject to her credit.

Lady Seton describes how personal losses and the subsequent search for service to others, led her to devote her life to bringing the joy of flowers to women all over the world.

My crisis came in 1947. The war had ended, my home had been bombed, I had lost my child and my husband did not return from the war. All my hopes and aspirations for the future had gone and I began to wonder why this had happened to me.

In this kind of situation you are standing at a crossroad where you have a choice of direction. You can either go down the road to self-pity, which is negative and non-productive or you can turn in the opposite direction and go forward, looking positively for life's meaning and what is meant for you personally. I settled for the latter.

I told myself I was only a tiny speck in the great universe ruled by a power greater than we recognize and perhaps there was some other work He wanted me to do. So I drew up a balance sheet. I knew only too well what to put on the debit side; then on the credit side I wrote that I had two good arms and two good legs (which many others had not), I had a certain ability and I desperately wanted to do something to help others less fortunate.

That was fine, but I had no particular qualifications. True, I had an interest in growing things and had been a recipient of the welcome packets of seeds sent over to us during the war by the Garden Clubs of America, but paradoxically that was responsible, in the short term, for another complication of my problem. After speaking at a luncheon in New York to say 'thank you' to our kind American friends – there were 280 presidents of Garden Clubs present – I was pressed to stay and accept a well-paid job in the States.

For me, this could not be the answer. I wanted so much to help put the world right in whatever small way might be indicated to me and I needed a sign. I had to refuse their attractive offer. Then, one day there came a call from the Kent Area of Women's Institutes, asking me to speak at a meeting of 900 members. I accepted, but when I arrived I was appalled at the sight of these women.

They shuffled into the hall, drab, down-at-heel and dispirited, showing all the signs of the deprivation of the war years and their attendant rationing. Rationing in those early postwar days meant shortage of nourishment, clothes and all commodities, no home decorating, house-painting or anything other than 'make do and mend'. These women needed to be inspired, to gain some means of expression and to have some new aim to bring colour back into their lives and their homes.

I looked at the audience and, pondering over my prepared speech, I knew it would not do. I knew I must say something more positive – something that would give them hope – and an objective that all of them could strive for and achieve. Inwardly, I cried out for guidance and when I stood up to speak the answer came to me in a flash. 'Flowers!' I cried out. 'Everyone of you can be an artist with flowers. Just think of the great variety of shapes and sizes there are. Think of the different colours and how they vary with the seasons – the palette for the artist in us is inexhaustible – and the materials are in abundance and never rationed.'

On the platform was the customary bowl of flowers. I took some and started to demonstrate several 'design pictures' with them, to illustrate my point. The result was electric. I became like an evangelist, hardly stopping for breath, and when I had finished speaking I was surrounded by ladies asking me to speak at their various meetings. That night I sat down quietly on my bed, looked up and said, 'Thank you, I know now where I am going.'

A great deal of hard work followed, travelling all over the country around the bombed cities, preaching and inspiring others to gain expression through flowers. I never had a moment's doubt that I could succeed, nor did I give a thought to the economics. When the flash of inspiration comes, it is for a reason and you are surely given all the help you need to succeed. If you believe in your inner self there is no limit to possible achievement.

To get my own message across to the full, I had to learn to write. Carried on by my enthusiasm and the determination of my crusade I worked at it and produced my first book, the sales of which by far exceeded the publisher's estimate. My writings, teachings and demonstrations have since led me all over the world, taking the message of flowers into schools, churches, hospitals and wherever there is a need.

The more I travel, the more I feel that perhaps flowers have a greater role to play in the affairs of the world than we realize.

They have a universal language and are understood by all, no matter what race, colour or creed. I often wish politicians and statesmen would have more flowers along their conference tables. I am sure there would be more goodwill and mutual understanding if they faced each other across a bowl of flowers, for they set us human beings such a fine example. For, despite their various sizes, shapes and colour, they do not seem to show jealousies, nor do they appear to fight for supremacy. They just seem to grow to give love and beauty to all who see them.

Even when I work twelve to fourteen hours a day, I love every minute of it. I have made no money but I am rich – rich in health and spirit. Looking back to that rainy day in Kent forty years ago, when I recognized and accepted the challenge, I am glad I did, for in giving out to others I completely forgot my own losses and became fulfilled. Life is full of obstacles, but they are there to be overcome. They are there to test us, to help us to grow spiritually.

So, whatever befalls you in life, accept it and look ahead. You do not know what is in store, but He knows what is within you, so be calm, be still and be guided.

Catherine Cookson OBE MA

Now in her eighties, Catherine Cookson is one of our most prolific and interesting authoresses. Her books reflect the age and the atmosphere in which she was brought up and will preserve for posterity a record of the difficulties of life in the North-East in the early years of the century. There can be no finer example of standing up to the difficulties of everyday existence than the life of Catherine Cookson and she has kindly allowed us to quote the following passage from her biographical book *Our Kate*. It deals with her mental breakdown in her forties.

∞∞∞∞∞∞∞∞∞∞∞∞∞

When it was suggested that perhaps I should see a psychiatrist, the boil burst. When, during my visit to him, this man further suggested that I should go for voluntary treatment, fear ran riot. Seeing this, he said it was up to me. I could either handle the situation myself, or have help. He was a very wise man in putting the onus on me for I knew I was no longer capable of handling this situation. It had now grown to such a gigantic form that even when in the state of deep depression, when nothing mattered, fear still held domination. I went as a voluntary patient for treatment.

When I had been in the place five weeks I went into Hereford on my own for the day. It was a test. The test proved to myself that I was still mentally ill. On the following Sunday I decided to go to Mass. The priest was coming out from

Hereford, the nice priest. I was clutching once more at the God I was denying, anything to use as a life-belt. I never forget the look on the priest's face when he saw me coming into that room. He came towards me, saying slowly, 'What-on-earth-are-you-doing *here*?'

A condition such as mine is difficult to explain at this distance. I can only say that I wouldn't wish the devil in hell to have a breakdown. And if I had the choice of having a crippling, agonising physical disease, or that of a breakdown, I know, without hesitation, which I would choose.

Fear had been my companion since a tiny child. Hardly ever a day went past but I feared something, and the accumulation of all those fears was with me now. FEAR... FEAR... FEAR... On with the years, mounting, swelling, until my laughter and small talk could not stretch to cover it, until I laughed too much. Then for a long period I laughed not at all.

I turned into a solid block of fear.

It would, at times, paralyze me, and I would lose the entire use of my legs; at others, it would make me retch for hours on end.

For 20 hours of each day I was in a wide-awake state of trembling terror, and the worst part of the state was the fear of what I might do in retaliation. The aggressiveness of my childhood period had returned.

If it wasn't for the terrible torment endured through a breakdown it would be good for everyone to experience it, for no state is so self-revealing.

All during this time of trial Tom had been wonderful with me. I wanted sympathy from no one else but him, and this was bad, and we both knew it, but it seemed that I had only him in the whole wide world. So, feeling like this, I don't know from where I dragged the courage to tell him not to sympathize with me; and when he took me at my word, being a woman, I blamed him. I felt, once again, lost and completely alone. But now he had hurt my pride, and this acted as a spur to make me fight all the harder against my condition. To be beholden to no one, to do it on my own.

I knew by this time, too, that I was not alone in my mental agony, the War was beginning to take its toll on nerves, and so I wrote my second broadcast, calling it, 'Putting nerves in their place'. My first broadcast had been called 'Learning to draw at thirty'.

It was strange how I first managed to get on the wireless; it all happened because I was annoyed. A lady made a remark, in public, half in fun and wholly in earnest, about the carrying quality of my voice. And as I was going home the thought came to me: I'll get on the wireless; I'll show her where my voice can carry me. And that is how it started. Each morning for three months, when Tom had gone to school, I took the script that I had written, about learning to draw, into the study, and, sitting opposite the electric light switch, I waited for it to turn red, because, I understood that's what happened in a broadcasting studio. When I thought I could read the script well enough for the BBC I sent it up, and to my surprise was asked to go for an audition. And I was on.

And now, I thought, I'm going to kill two birds with one stone. I'm going to get rid of the fear of anyone knowing I've had a breakdown by speaking of it, and in doing it I will help others, because I realized that many people were suffering as much from the fact that anyone should know that they had had a breakdown as from the trouble itself. But even knowing this, the result of the broadcast was astounding. I had letters from all kinds of people, all suffering. Moreover, many people came to see me, people who couldn't believe that I was in the same state as themselves. They imagined that I could, at one time, have felt as terrible as they did, but they could not believe that I was still feeling like this, for a good part of the time anyway.

So, on the days when I hit bottom again and felt I just couldn't go on, I would remember certain people to whom my apparently peaceful mental condition was as a lodestone, and they, in their turn, would help me to go on with the fight.

I was helped, too, at this time very much by the writings of Leslie Weatherhead. So much did he help me that I wrote him a letter of thanks and was amazed to get a reply by return of post, thanking me in turn for giving him a bright start on a dull Monday morning. I was puzzled by this until I learned through his further writings that he, too, knew all there was to know about breakdowns.

I look back now on the years between forty and fifty as on a painful nightmare. Not only had I my mental state to contend with but the inevitable attack on all sections of my weakened system by an early menopause. Add to this, neuritis of the arms and legs, a skin allergy, and the capacity for picking up anything that was going, even mange from my bull terrier, to say nothing of my nose, which, if possible, was bleeding more at this time, and had also taken on to itself a painful antrum.

My doctor used to infuriate me, for, no matter what I went to him with, he would say airily, 'Oh, Mrs Cookson! you've got to expect this, it's your temperament, you know. You've got to pay for being a writer.'

In 1948, '49 and '50 I had three operations on my temperament. I may say here that these were the first operations for which, before I went down to the theatre I was given an injection to quieten the system. Four out of the previous six times I had been in an operating theatre I had lain on the table while they cleared up the gore from the last patient. It's odd how people always thought I was tough.

Following this, my temperament gave me, with the help of some tree shears, mastitis of the breasts. Then my temperament, with the help of my pen, gave me writer's cramp, and neuritis which caused a frozen shoulder. Some temperament!

Baroness Cox

Raised to the peerage in 1983, Caroline Cox began her career as a student nurse at the London Hospital. She subsequently worked as a Staff Nurse at Edgware General Hospital until she was admitted for six months as a patient with TB. While convalescing, she studied for London University external degrees in social science and was then appointed to the Department of Sociology at the Polytechnic of North London, where she progressed from Lecturer to Head of Department. She then became Director of the Nursing Education Research Unit at Chelsea College in the University of London from 1977–83. She is currently a Patron of the Medical Aid for Poland Fund, Chairman of the Jagiellonian Trust, Chairman of the Education Study Group at the Centre for Policy Studies, Chairman of the Parental Alliance for Choice in Education and Chairman of the Academic Council for Peace and Freedom; and she serves on the Management Committee of St Christopher's Hospice. Baroness Cox is married to Dr Murray Cox, FRC Psych, and has two sons and one daughter.

It happened last year in Sudan. My son Jonathan was working there with a Christian organization – having trained as a nurse in order to work in less developed countries. In one of his letters he said that there was an acute shortage of nurses, especially over the summer. So I offered my services – and was accepted, despite my age!

I duly arrived in Khartoum and was sent to work in what was generally reckoned to be a tough assignment in the desert three hundred kilometres west of Khartoum. I went, with a Canadian nurse, to a remote township called Hamrat El-Wiz, in an area which has been devastated by drought and famine. We were to develop a health programme consisting of health education and immunization for mothers and children.

Health education can save many lives. For example, many babies and children die of diarrhoea because parents do not realize the importance of giving them plenty to drink to avoid death from dehydration. And many more lives can be saved by the immunization project we were to set up. This would provide protection from six killer diseases: diphtheria, measles, poliomyelitis, tetanus, whooping cough and tuberculosis.

Our work took us beyond our little township into many remote outlying villages. Travel was quite hazardous as there were no roads or even tracks. Also, we had no radio contact between Hamrat El-Wiz and Khartoum, nor between our vehicles and base when we were out in the desert – so if we had a breakdown (which we frequently did) we were stranded and had to make our way back as best we could – on one occasion, Katherine and I had to resort to a five-hour camel ride to reach the safety of 'home' again.

On the day about which I am writing, we went to one village, where the Sheikh gave us a warm welcome. After we had finished our work there, we asked the direction to our next destination – a village called Mahbis. The Sheikh said it was too far to give directions and sent one of his elders with us as a guide.

We set off over very rough terrain. Some of it was mountainous and very rocky. This alternated with deep dried-up river beds, or wadis, as they are known. These were very difficult to negotiate. The sides were almost perpendicular and the sand was very soft. We had to use the bottom gear in order to get the Land Rover to plough its way out. Sometimes it seemed as if it would not make it.

Five times we had to go into these wadis. We would emerge with relief and set off over more hills. After two hours, we asked our guide how much further we had to go. He said it was still quite a way – beyond the next mountain. We began to get a little worried as there was no sign of any village anywhere on the horizon and we did not want to be stranded in the desert when darkness came.

Suddenly, disaster struck. We were going at considerable speed when the terrain changed and we hit some rocks. In a split second we were thrown about, everything in the back of the vehicle catapulted out, we lost all our drinking water and the Land Rover packed up.

This was a bad moment. The loss of water was very serious indeed, as the heat is intense – at over 140° in the sun, thirst sets in very quickly. In the circumstances, there was nothing we could do except to try to get the vehicle going again as quickly as possible. The engine could be started up but the wheels would not move. We had to do several repairs, including transferring brake fluid into the hydraulic clutch. We were still working when it became too dark to see properly. We resigned ourselves to a thirsty night and an uncertain morrow. It was at this moment that an Arab appeared out of nowhere on a camel. Our first, desperate question was 'Is there water in the wadi?' Miraculously, there was – the only wadi with water for a hundred kilometres. We filled our containers with water which was black and full of all manner of strange things – but we made a fire of scrubwood and boiled it, to avoid poisoning.

We then settled for what sleep we could get and as soon as dawn broke we began to work again on the Land Rover. Eventually, after three hours, we managed to reassemble it. The engine started but, to our dismay, the wheels refused to turn. Now, we thought, we really are stranded. There was no vehicle back at Hamrat capable of coming to rescue us; and, even if there had been, our friends could not have found us, as there were no tracks visible over the rocks and shifting sand.

The obvious practical task was to boil more water before the heat of the sun became really oppressive. I turned to tend the fire, when suddenly I heard the Land Rover moving. Our interpreter had been praying intensely and felt moved to try to drive in *high* gears. Sure enough, it worked. But we then had to make the agonizing decision whether to abandon the source of our water and attempt the treacherous return journey, only able to use high gear. This carried the risk of getting stuck in one of the dried-up wadis, where we would soon come to a thirsty end. Or we could stay where we were, with the advantage of water but no prospect of rescue.

We prayed and decided to try to make the return journey, carrying as much water as possible. We will never forget that journey: the acute anxiety as we approached each of those steep wadis and the relief as the Land Rover pulled out time and again. We prayed each time, and it felt as if someone – God – just picked the Land Rover up and lifted it out.

In such situations, when we turn to prayer, we must pray 'Thy will be done.' On the morning we left, my prayer book had an excerpt from T. S. Eliot with the phrase 'the death in the desert'. I wondered whether God was trying to prepare us! But in the event, we were spared to return to base alive – and full of gratitude for, in John Wesley's famous phrase, 'so many journeying mercies.'

Constance Cummings CBE

Although born and brought up in the United States, Constance Cummings has spent most of her professional life in the UK, in radio, TV, films and the theatre. A member of the Arts Council from 1965–71 and Chairman of the Young People's Theatre Panel 1966–70, she joined the National Theatre Company in 1971. Since 1978 she has been a Council member of the English Stage Company.

Her theatre appearances include *Goodbye Mr. Chips, The Taming of the Shrew, St Joan, Fallen Angels, Hamlet, The Chalk Garden, Coriolanus, The Cherry Orchard* and many others. In 1986 she travelled all over England with her one-woman show about Fanny Kemble, the Victorian actress.

Happily married for forty years to the late Benn Levy MBE, she has one son and one daughter.

∞∞∞∞∞∞∞∞∞∞∞∞∞∞∞

When I was a child my mother and I lived on the coast of California. We used to swim in the sea almost every day that I was not in school.

There was a rip tide which could occur along that stretch of coast; it did not happen very often but when it did it was truly dangerous. A strong flow of water swept back underneath the waves and anything caught in it could be swept a long distance out to sea before surfacing.

One day when I was about eleven years old – a lovely summer morning – my mother and I were swimming some distance apart and I realized she was in trouble, she was struggling to keep afloat, and then I felt the undertow pulling at my legs and feet and I knew what was happening to her.

I shouted to her to be strong and I started to swim towards her, at the same time trying to wave to the shore to get attention and help.

It seems strange when I remember it all for I was only a child and my mother was a very good swimmer, but she was obviously in some unusual difficulty. I was terribly frightened as I felt the water trying to suck me down to the bottom – but not for myself, for her! My concern for her gave me a strength beyond myself and I managed to get to her and keep her on top of the waves until two men who had been sunbathing on the shore got out to us and floated her to the beach. There she was given first aid as she was so exhausted and had swallowed so much sea water.

It was not until much later when I could bear to think about it all that I realized what strength and perhaps courage is given to us when we are struggling, not for ourselves but for someone else. This discovery has been affirmed for me many times in my life.

Robin Day
OBE RDI ARCA FSIAD

Robin Day is a leading design consultant. He has designed seating for many auditoria, including the Royal Festival Hall, Royal Shakespeare Theatre, Stratford, and the Barbican Arts Centre. Other commissions include the interior design of the Super VC10 and other aircraft and furniture which is made or sold in over fifty countries. He has sat on juries for many national and international design competitions. He has six Design Centre Awards, gold and silver medals for Milan Triennale exhibits and the SIAD Design Medal.

Robin Day is married to Lucienne Day RDI, who is also a distinguished design consultant and they have one daughter.

∞∞∞∞∞∞∞∞∞∞∞∞∞∞

I suppose that few people who, like me, have lived for over seventy years have escaped at least one severe set back in the form of accidents or illness.

Two such incidents come to my mind. One was a dramatic mountaineering accident which almost killed me, but which in a strange way caused me less suffering than others who were involved. The occasion was on the face of a 500 feet high rock precipice. We had ascended to about half way up this crag to where the rock was vertical and holdless. Progress was only possible by a 'hand traverse' which I was to lead, whilst my second was securely belayed to the rock some twenty feet below. This traverse consisted of a horizontal crack for the fingers only, with no holds at all for one's boots. Somewhere along this pitch I fell off – how or why, I shall never know, as concussion obliterated a short space of memory. Instead of plummetting 250 feet to the rocks below, the rope held and I hung unconscious and upside down with a fractured skull, bleeding profusely and some forty feet below my climbing partner. I learned later that I was eventually lowered to the foot of the cliff by a rescue team and taken to hospital by helicopter.

Awareness of my own problems only really began on surfacing to consciousness in the casualty ward the next day. Pain and appalling headaches were to be with me for many days, and I suppose anxiety about the possible long-term effects of brain damage. However, concussion had shielded me from the trauma on the mountain. This was experienced by my companion secured at one end of the rope to the mountain, while I hung out of sight and possibly dead on the rope below. This experience was so devastating that, sadly, this person did not climb again for many years. It was hard also for my wife who, on the phone to the hospital, was told to travel north through the night as, 'you never know how long people with severe head injuries may live'! Thus, one's errors, misjudgments or weaknesses can be really rough on others. For me, it was just a period of waiting. The relaxation of climbing mountains was important to me at that time and I was determined to return to this sport just as soon as I could, and to this end I surreptitiously exercised while still in bed. At first just hands and fingers, using springs, and later arms, until at last I could stand again and increase mobility. Before another year was over I was back in the hills with only the occasional severe headache as a reminder.

Three years ago a much more commonplace incident gave me greater cause for fear and despondency. Although feeling fit and well at the time, haemorrhage led to the diagnosis of cancer of the colon and the need for a major and urgent operation. I was surprised rather than shocked, and a little angry that this should be happening to me – a stupid sentiment as thousands of people have the same problem.

With an extensive abdominal operation, there is a lot which is frightening, messy and depressing, such as emerging from the anaesthetic, shattered, immobilized and sprouting tubes carrying blood, glucose, waste and so on.

On regaining consciousness, one lives for a time in a dim and shaky world followed by the splendid realization that the crucial part is over – the evil growth has been cut out – and that now one must dig in and will one's feeble body to gain strength and recover.

In a strange way, in spite of the pain and mess, I look back on this period in hospital as a happy one. I felt so privileged to be alive, and with a fresh vision saw everyday things for the miracles which they really are. My bed was by a large window, and I marvelled at the great changing patterns of the clouds in the sky and the intricate and inventive structure of the trees on the courtyard. My awareness of people, too, seemed heightened. The good nature of other suffering people in the ward, and especially the extraordinary kindness and patience of the nurses and staff. Perhaps this euphoria is common.

With post-operative weakness I had my moments of deep depression but, overall, I knew that life was wonderful and that I had to make myself get strong again to live it fully. I found myself working mentally on new design projects, and as soon as I could raise myself a little I asked for a sketch book and was able to carry this work forward. Other diversions were trying to get away without taking the usual painkillers and sleeping tablets. In one way or another my complete recovery was accelerated and I was soon back working, and ski-mountaineering in Arctic Lapland with no serious after-effects and the reassurance that the cancer would probably not return.

Once again I had been lucky. Although ancient, I seemed to have had the advantage of a resilient constitution and activities that I was intent on resuming and, best of all, a wife and daughter giving me wonderful encouragement and support every single day after the surgery.

It seems to me that we can gain from really stressful experiences. They jolt us into another level of consciousness. At least, that is what happened to me. We become blunted by the daily routine of life and take it all for granted, whereas life and this planet we live on is rich and full of wonder. I can't always retain this impression – it is easy to slip back into unawareness or even pessimism. I sometimes just have to remember the positive, constructive and even exciting experience of moving bit by bit and day by day from a carved-up feeble wreck to fully restored normality.

Shirley Anne Field

Shirley Anne Field began her career in the theatre before making her name as a film actress in a series of successes including *Dry Rot*, *The Entertainer*, *Saturday Night and Sunday Morning*, *Doctor in Clover* and *Alfie*. Her most recent film, *My Beautiful Launderette*, has also been screened on television.

We are particularly pleased that she should contribute to this book, as one who can paint a true and loving picture of the National Children's Home.

It was during the war, I was a baby girl and, together with my little brother, was too young to be evacuated, like most children, to live with families outside London. For a number of reasons my mother was unable to care for us in addition to our two elder sisters, so we were sent to a baby home on the south coast. My mother came to see us when we were settled in and knew we were better looked after than we could have been at home.

When I was too big to stay there the Matron wrote to the National Children's Home and so, at the age of five, I was sent from one end of the country to the other – from Sussex to the National Children's Home at Edgeworth in Lancashire, leaving my brother behind.

For a five-year old little girl this was a terrifying and shattering experience – the sort of experience from which you recover as time goes by, but which you never forget. When they put me on the train I thought my mother and my two elder sisters would be there at the other end of the journey to meet me, but of course they were not. It was an apparently thoughtless decision to send me so far away when they had a branch of the Home in the south. Perhaps they thought I would be safer and less susceptible to outside influence, as it was a two-day journey for my mother to get there from London and anyway, the fare was more than she could afford.

It was like being in a vacuum in those first weeks at Edgeworth. Although we were separated we were a very close, loving family and I missed them all terribly. What is more, my southern accent made me different from all the others; their Lancashire dialect was strange to me and I felt an outcast. At that time I badly needed confidence and I used to talk about my family to try and establish myself as a person. But I would be told, 'Now, don't make up stories, Shirley – you don't have a mother and two sisters.' That used to upset me terribly. I needed to be believed and accepted. I wanted desperately to be back where I came from – wherever that was, I wanted to be back. The fact that we were poor and our home had very little comfort did not matter. I wanted to be back with my family. I could not settle down.

All kinds of children, from all kinds of families and for all kinds of reasons came into that Home – and indeed many enjoyed a life they had never known before. But children in that situation all share one thing, they need to be regarded as equal members of society and not a thing apart, and the first essential is to give them understanding. Fortunately, the attitude in the Home today is vastly different, especially in that particular respect, but in many other ways the treatment we received was really lovely – and loving – and I am sure will never change.

When we grow up we know that sudden changes cause misery to children – homesickness in particular – but that time brings new hopes and new joys. Two things happened to change life for me. Firstly, my young brother came to the Home and secondly, I experienced my first real Christmas. At home we had never celebrated Christmas in the traditional way, we were far too poor – and this first Christmas at Edgeworth was a magical experience for me. Four hundred children all waiting for Father Christmas, who was, of course, the Governor (as he was called) dressed up for the part. This was the first time I had ever seen big Christmas trees – there were huge trees all through the Home and we all had wonderful presents donated by generous and kind people. I had never had presents like that before in all my life – and the love, joy and affection that I recognized then, opened my eyes to the life the Home offered. Despite the Victorian Gothic buildings and all the faults inevitable in an institution, my Home would compare favourably with any public school, and for one very good reason, as I came to know. The Home was fuelled by love and religion. Things went wrong, of course they did, but there was a backbone of faith, truth and humility and they did their best.

There were moments of supreme joy, as well as of sorrow. These people, the Governor and the Sisters, had given their lives and their love to God, Jesus and the children, and paradoxically enough, it was because of this faith, this sweetness, that things sometimes went wrong. You have to remember that the little Sisters who looked after us earned only two pounds per month and were happy with that. To them the work was a vocation. All the staff were very well-meaning. There were those genteel Methodist Sisters, missionaries' daughters, some of them, who would try to bring the standards of their own homes to these deprived children. I will always remember Sister Nancy, who used to make up little presents for me because I did not have any sent from outside. My mother had, by then, gone to America to get married again and I had lost touch with her and my sisters. Sister Nancy cared deeply and understood, and when she read out the pocket money list she would add threepence out of her own monthly two pounds so that I should not be different from the others.

On our birthdays we were allowed to have our own little party with three of our special friends invited. It was wartime, everything was rationed and in short supply but Sister Nancy would make us cocoa and little fairy cakes, which we sat and ate inside the upturned laundry box – which she organized to give us a sense of occasion and a little privacy. If anyone didn't have any presents she would always buy little gifts out of her own money. She was an angel.

Looking back at my childhood in perspective I count myself lucky. My mother wanted to take me and my younger brother with her when she went to America, but having regard to the circumstances and with, according to their beliefs, the best interests of us children at heart, the Home refused to let us go. I was devastated at the time, but as it turned out the decision was the right one. Had we gone, we would have been living in the deep South, in comparative poverty, and would have been denied the upbringing and the opportunities open to us as we grew up in England. I had a far better education and I owe my good health today to that background. We were safe, where we were, brought up in a strict Methodist society, with beliefs, standards and rules of behaviour that were unbending. This creed and code of living was strictly observed by all, you knew where you stood and that experience has served me well all my adult life.

Dennis Flanders RWS RBA

One of our foremost artists working in pencil and watercolour, Dennis Flanders is famed for his townscapes and landscapes. Educated at Merchant Taylors' School, followed by evening classes at the Regent Street Polytechnic, he quickly became known for his drawings in the national and provincial Press and for eight years (1956-64) he was one of the special artists of the Illustrated London News.

He has drawings in the National War Collection (1939-45), the Guildhall Library, the Bank of England, the National Library of Wales and hundreds of his pictures hang in private houses around the country and abroad.

Dennis Flanders is married and has one son and one daughter. His wife Dalma is a bookbinder and designer.

∞∞∞∞∞∞∞∞∞∞∞∞∞

This is the story of a young man who suddenly knew - in a flash - that he must throw up his job and engage in the career for which he had a special gift. My road to Damascus was, in fact, no further than Oxford Street and I was twenty-one at the time.

I was the son of a musician father and an artist mother and enjoyed a traditional education at Merchant Taylors' School. I had, ever since I could remember, been quite good at drawing - a gift no doubt handed down from my mother - and, indeed, at the age of seven, I had been awarded the Princess Louise Gold Medal of the Royal Drawing Society.

My natural bent would have been to devote myself to an artistic career. However, for people in the world of art and music, things were very difficult in the 1930s and my father was no exception. For his son to elect to try to make a living from drawing would be quite unthinkable. I was expected to go into an office, as most middle class children of that period were expected to do and although the thought of it was quite unbearable to me, I did, in effect, do so. For two whole years I worked in the office of a chartered accountant in Walbrook in the City, but I was, throughout, determined to get into the art world by hook or by crook.

But how to begin, and earn a living at the same time? That was the burning question. It is a curious thing that when you want sufficiently to achieve something and are single-minded enough, the opportunity will sooner or later present itself. I had already thrown off the shackles of accountancy and was working for a firm of interior decorators – a job I got through the advertisements in the *Daily Telegraph*. Here there was a certain amount of art work to be done, but I needed to learn methods of production and that meant another change. Back to the columns of the *Daily Telegraph*, and I found a job with a printer in Farringdon Road.

This was a timely opportunity. It was September and the job was to draw houses and animals for personalized Christmas cards. People would send in photographs of Fido or their house in Esher and I would have to copy these on to zinc plates with a 9H pencil. Wonderful new experience – but the market for Christmas cards does not extend into the New Year and in January I found myself employed in making ruled lines for the pages of ledgers. This was a soul-destroying occupation and death to a creative artist, and just when my morale was at its lowest I had the Damascus experience.

One lunchtime, walking in Oxford Street I came to the window of Bumpus' bookshop (now no more) and was immediately transfixed. I found myself looking at about a dozen magnificent reproductions of drawings, the like of which I had never seen before. They were by the celebrated Muirhead Bone and their subject matter was the towns, cathedrals, palaces and people of Spain; they were pages of a book shortly to be published. The splendour of these drawings was something quite beyond my experience at that time. 'This is the stuff for me,' I said to myself – 'but why Spain?' And then I knew. Then and there I made up my mind to do the same for England.

There was no alternative. I had to have my freedom. But I was terrified of handing in my notice, my poor father would have been angry and disappointed. We had very little money at that time. So I started making ghastly mistakes in my ledger ruling and duly got the sack. My father, to my relief, accepted the situation as a *fait accompli* and did not even reproach me. Maybe he was not entirely surprised; after all, my mother was a painter too.

Now I was in a pickle. I had lost my job and was left with a consuming ambition but no prospects. What I now needed, most urgently, was a sense of direction and an opportunity. Both presented themselves. I had, some time before, been introduced to Hanslip Fletcher, whose lovely drawings in *The Sunday Times*, of London and other towns, I had long admired and I now decided to follow his lead and draw for the Press.

My opportunity came in the shape of the Bishop of Barking, our local prelate, who was to retire and give up his home, a rather lovely early 19th century building in Walthamstow. I asked the Bishop's permission to draw the house, which he graciously gave. The local paper reproduced my pen and ink drawing, the local museum bought it, the Bishop's son also ordered replicas for his family. In one fortnight I had earned, freelance, three times what I would have made had I stayed in that prosaic printing works in the Farringdon Road.

The spell was broken. I had proved to myself and my family that I could make a livelihood at what I did best. The opening battle was won.

My working life since than has been a joyful and satisfying voyage and the goal I set myself fifty years before, was achieved in 1984. That year saw the publication of *Dennis Flanders' Britannia*, a collection of 224 reproductions of my best drawings, recording the splendour of traditional Britain.

Christina Foyle

The daughter of William Foyle, founder of the world's best known bookselling organization, Christina Foyle has devoted her life to the promotion of literature. For over fifty years she has held the famous Foyle's Literary Luncheons, where book lovers have been able to meet and hear great personalities.

During the 1939-45 war Foyle's bookshop all but succumbed in the bombing of London and here Christina Foyle tells of her reactions to the devastation and the encouragement from so many quarters which enabled the firm to survive.

Looking back on my life, which has been very fortunate and happy, there have been few crises. The saddest times have been the deaths of beloved friends, many of whom grew up with me and were killed in the war.

I think that perhaps the great crisis in my life came in the year 1940. Before that, in the 1930s, I was a carefree irresponsible girl. Life was wonderful then. London was a beautiful city and people were elegant. It was safe to go anywhere alone, day or night.

My days were spent enjoying life at Foyles, meeting fascinating people – Bernard Shaw, H. G. Wells, Elinor Glyn – and my nights dancing, or attending the plays of Noel Coward and Ivor Novello.

Then came the war, which started for Londoners with the

Blitz of 1940. I really grew up in September 1940 and by May 1941 my hair had turned grey.

In the first great raid on London a huge bomb tore a hole in the Charing Cross Road just outside the shop. We looked into the horrifying crater and saw something moving. It was a Canadian soldier, quite drunk, but still alive.

All the windows at Foyles were shattered, the doors hanging on their hinges and the place smothered in dust. Two publishers' representatives surveyed the scene. One said to the other, 'Poor Willie Foyle. He will never survive this.'

'Won't he?' I thought.

The bombing continued night after night, and many of the staff could not stand the strain and left. London was a stricken and deserted city and we had very few customers. No one, who was not compelled to, came to London and soon we had difficulty in paying our accounts. We owed money to everyone – the bank, the publishers, the Post Office – and life became a nightmare.

My days were spent calling on publishers, begging them to hold over their accounts. I spent hours with the bank manager, who was very eccentric. He collected picture postcards and would show me his prize exhibits. If I admired his taste and perception in the collection of the cards and flattered him enough, he would increase our overdraft very generously. The Post Office, too, were very kind.

After the dreary days of fobbing off creditors came the nights listening to the bombs. 1940 was the worst year of my life. And then, with spring of 1941 things became a little easier. The air raids were not so intense. People began to come to London again and, most wonderful of all, everyone wanted books. Then started the great demand for books, which has continued until this day.

People wanted books on every subject – art, music, philosophy, cookery and so on. A new, much more educated public was emerging and a new age began for the book trade.

For me, it was a crisis overcome. Sometimes in that terrible year I used to think that Foyles would never survive and life for me without the bookshop was unthinkable.

The lesson I really learned was how good and kind and trusting people were and I shall never forget the help the publishers gave me – Collins, Heinemann, Hodder and many others – and dear kind Barclays Bank, who enabled us to carry on and survive a great ordeal.

The Rt. Rev.
The Bishop of Gibraltar in Europe

The Rev. John Satterthwaite, born in 1925, was educated at Millom Grammar School, Leeds University (BA) and the College of the Resurrection, Mirfield.

After two years as History Master at St Luke's School, Haifa, he became Curate of St Barnabas Church, Carlisle, and in 1954 came to London to work in Lambeth Palace with the Archbishop of Canterbury on the Church of England Council on Foreign Relations. He was General Secretary of the Council from 1959–70, and from 1965–70 also General Secretary of the Archbishop's Communion on Roman Catholic Relations.

In 1970 he was appointed Bishop Suffragan of Fulham (for North and Central Europe). The following year he was enthroned also as Bishop of Gibraltar for Southern Europe and Turkey and was known as the Bishop of Fulham and Gibraltar. The new diocese for all Europe was created in 1980.

The Bishop is an Hon. Canon of Utrecht and holds decorations from various foreign churches.

~~~~~~~~~~~~~~~~~~~~~~

Since I became a priest in 1950, my ministry has taken me to many parts of the world. I have visited all the countries behind the Iron Curtain, and even our little Christian community in

Ulan Bator in Outer Mongolia, and travel has not been without its moments. On one occasion, flying to Moscow from New Delhi via Baku on the Caspian and Erivan in Soviet Armenia I was stranded in Tashkent in a sandstorm. However, in all these years I have only once been apprehended and locked up in a Communist country – an experience which I would not wish on anyone.

It happened in East Berlin in the early sixties, soon after the building of the Berlin Wall. At the time I was working in Lambeth Palace as foreign adviser to the Archbishop of Canterbury, and Secretary-General of the Council on Foreign Relations – a midget 'Foreign Office' of the Church of England. The churches in East Germany were experiencing a most difficult time from the Government of the GDR and Archbishop Michael Ramsey was eager to give support for our Christian brethren beleaguered in East Berlin and East Germany. I was, accordingly, asked to take a message to Herr Ulbricht in East Berlin from the Archbishop of Canterbury asking for freedom of worship in the GDR.

After flying to West Berlin I crossed over into the east side of the city, and delivered my message at the office of Herr Ulbricht. I was received correctly, and allowed to go without any problem. Crossing back again to West Berlin I had a meeting that evening with Lutheran clergy there and stayed one more night before continuing my journey to Warsaw, where I was due to take services at the British Embassy on the following Sunday. Next day, as there were no flights to Warsaw, I left West Berlin by train, to cross to Poland through East Germany. The first station in East Berlin then was Friedrichstrasse. When we arrived there the entire train was searched by East German guards. Two young soldiers marched me off the train with a pistol held in my back, accusing me of travelling on a passport which was 'out of order'! They took me to a cell-like room in the station and locked me in. At that period it was common for clergy travelling between the West and East to be harrassed for no apparent reason. My passport was in no way at fault.

This was my first experience of incarceration and my mind was filled with horror. It was impossible to contact a soul... There were then no diplomatic relations between East Germany and Great Britain, and I wondered how long I would be left to languish in a Communist gaol. Prayer does not come easily to many people until there is a certain stress and my own prayers had been feeble, but at that moment I realized what prayer could mean. After a while of being left to my own devices I suddenly felt a great calm, and knew there was a force greater than myself, and of those who held me. Any sense of panic now vanished and I was left with a feeling of firm support.

About 4.30 a.m. next morning a more senior East German officer came to interrogate me and I explained that someone from the British Embassy in Warsaw would soon be going to meet me from the train I was supposed to be arriving on from Berlin. Within half an hour another officer appeared and told me I could leave and get back to West Berlin as best I could. I was free!

When they released me I found myself in company with a middle-aged Pole who was freed at the same time. After serving with the Free Polish Army he had settled in the U.K. but having lost his wife he was on his way to see her family in Poland. The experience had unnerved him badly. He was in a very highly nervous condition and I was glad to be able to befriend him.

As trains on the S-Bahn (underground) ran all night I collected the Pole's baggage and my own, and managed to steer him and myself and all our belongings on to the train – free of the help of any East Germans. At the Zoo Station in West Berlin we left the train and went through the barrier without tickets – as we were 'refugees'. I was able to get a taxi and take my Polish companion back to the hotel where I had previously stayed, and see him properly looked after.

In retrospect it was clear that my own fright and panic was

little compared with the state of my newly acquired Polish friend, and I realized that my own arrest and ordeal was well worth it, if it meant giving help to someone in greater need at that time.

Beryl Grey CBE DMus DLitt

Prima Ballerina with the Royal Ballet (formerly Sadler's Wells Ballet) from 1942–57, Beryl Grey left to become a freelance ballerina. She won the distinction of being the first Western ballerina to appear with the Bolshoi Ballet in Moscow, Leningrad, Kiev and Tiflis and the first Western ballerina to dance with the Chinese Ballet Company in Peking and Shanghai. Also, in the period 1958–64, she made regular guest appearances with the Royal Ballet at Covent Garden and on tours in Africa, the USA and the Far East. From 1968–79 she was Artistic Director of the London Festival Ballet. She has written two books, *Red Curtain Up* and *Through the Bamboo Curtain*.

Beryl Grey holds a number of prominent appointments in the world of dancing, including Presidency of the Dance Council of Wales, Vice-Presidency of the Royal Academy of Dancing, Chairman of the Imperial Society of Teachers of Dancing. She is also a Trustee of the Royal Ballet Benevolent Fund, Dance Teachers' Benevolent Fund and a Governor of London City Ballet.

Beryl Grey is married to Dr Svenson and has one son, Ingvar.

I was a 'baby ballerina', which was quite unusual in England. I joined the Royal Ballet (then the Sadler's Wells Ballet) in 1941 at the age of fourteen, dancing in one-act ballets and from my fifteenth birthday in 1942 I danced leading roles in the full-length classics. My career progressed steadily and I had great hopes for my future.

After the war the Company re-opened the Royal Opera House, Covent Garden and I naturally expected to dance the lead in *The Sleeping Beauty*, sharing it with Margot Fonteyn, Moira Shearer and Pamela May. It was then that the bottom dropped out of my world. Ninette de Valois, the Director of the Ballet, informed me that I had grown too tall for the leading Princess Aurora role and that I must be content to dance the secondary role of The Lilac Fairy, which she considered more suited to my height.

I was bitterly disappointed and although I loved dancing The Lilac Fairy and worked hard to achieve a big success, I was not prepared to accept the ruling – which would seriously limit my prospects within the Company. I determined to learn the role to perfection regardless of not being allowed to dance it in performance. The Lilac Fairy only dances in the first Act and the rest of the time she walks and mimes and does the odd bourrée, so there was plenty of time for me to dance in the wings to the orchestra as it was playing. I practised every night at the back of that vast Covent Garden stage and as we gave nightly performances from January through to July, I knew the role perfectly.

One Thursday in June all three ballerinas fell ill and Ninette de Valois told me I was to dance Princess Aurora that very evening, which I did, to my great joy. Moreover I danced it again on the Friday and Saturday and all performances were a success. Thereafter I was accepted and I danced both roles and stayed with the Royal Ballet until 1957, when I left to become a freelance ballerina.

I think the important thing is never to accept what appears to be the inevitable defeat. Always be prepared – like a Boy Scout – build up on your talents and whatever experience or success you have acquired, confident that it will pay off at some time. And when that time comes, as it assuredly will –

and without warning – you will be ready to meet the challenge.

In the theatre – and especially in dancing – being prepared means one hundred per cent self-discipline. It is one of the few areas in the world where discipline is absolutely vital. And self-control. However experienced you may become, it is always a fresh challenge every time you go on the stage. You cannot go for even one day without practising and great attention has always to be paid to eating and many other habits. But it is a small price to pay for doing something you really want to do.

If you have faith in God and yourself, and are prepared to back up that faith with hard work and refuse to be put off, you will overcome the unexpected obstacles and win through.

Sir Charles Groves CBE FRCM

Born in 1915 and educated at St Paul's Cathedral Choir School, Sutton Valence School and the Royal College of Music, he joined the BBC in 1938 as Chorus Master of the Music Productions Unit. He rose to become Conductor of the BBC Revue Orchestra (1943) and of the BBC Northern Orchestra (1944–51). There followed a period of ten years in Bournemouth, including Conductor of the Bournemouth Symphony Orchestra (1954–61), and after two years as Resident Musical Director of the Welsh National Opera Company (1961–63) he became Musical Director and Resident Conductor of the Royal Liverpool Philharmonic Orchestra until 1977. During 1978–79 he was Musical Director of the English National Opera.

Sir Charles has been Associate Conductor of the Royal Philharmonic Orchestra since 1967 and President of the National Youth Orchestra of Great Britain from 1977. He has toured Australia, New Zealand, South Africa, North and South America, Japan and Europe. He is married and has three children.

I often reflect upon the good fortune that has enabled me to earn my living by doing something which I would cheerfully do year in and year out for pleasure. Music has brought me more happiness than I can measure but it also helped me to survive a period in my young life when I might well have gone under or to the bad.

I was born on 10 March 1915, the day of one of the bloodiest battles on the Somme, the battle of 'Neuve Chappelle'; I had almost arrived, as my mother was fond of telling me, in the bargain basement of Selfridge's store whither, I suppose, she had gone rather belatedly for something pertaining to my imminent arrival.

My father had been invalided out of the army, having contracted tuberculosis and almost my only memory of him is of his terrible coughing and his impatience with my poor mother, who was for ever up and down stairs in answer to his knocks on the bedroom floor with a heavy walking stick. He died in 1921, leaving us to get on with a very small army pension and some money left to mother by my grandfather.

We were only two, there had been an elder brother who had died when only a few days old, and we soon developed a wonderful relationship in which music was very important. I had started piano lessons at five years old and entered the choir of the local church when I was seven. Mother taught in the Sunday School and she and I used to play and sing together. It seemed to me to be a very happy life; I enjoyed my schooldays and made friends easily. Then, suddenly, the cloud of financial anxiety overshadowed us and my mother became worried about the future and how I was to be educated. Luckily my father's erstwhile boss was a member of a City Livery Company and suggested that I should enter the voice trial for choristers at St Paul's Cathedral. This I did in the autumn of 1923; I was one of two boys admitted and I joined the Choir School in January 1924.

Wrenched away from our happy home together, I suddenly found life very tough indeed and I can only guess how hard it was for my mother. I am sure that she did not look after herself as she should have done because in the spring of 1925 she went to bed one day with a severe chill; in twenty-four hours she was dead of septic pneumonia and I was left an orphan.

There followed months of misery beginning with a diphtheria epidemic in the country from which many people died. I was one of two St Paul's boys to catch it and spent thirteen weeks in an isolation hospital. At this time it was discovered that my mother had not left a will and there followed arguments between my late father's brothers and my mother's two sisters as to who should be my guardian. In the end I became a Ward in Chancery and my aunts looked after me until I was twenty-one.

Looking back on those Choir School days sixty years ago, I realize that I was a very lonely, disillusioned and bad-tempered boy, very often in trouble with the authorities and likely to become like David Copperfield, when he first went away to school and had to wear a placard on his back reading: 'Take care of him. He bites'. Then gradually, very gradually my musical gifts opened up a future for me and gave me back my pride and self respect.

My life since then has certainly not been roses all the way but the thread of music has been strong enough to keep me safe from the worst excesses of pride or despair. St Paul's Cathedral took the place of my father and mother because, although my two aunts were devoted to me, they were neither of them cut out to be able to cope with a boy of ten who had been suddenly thrust upon them. Although I did not follow the musical path pointed out for me by the Choir School, I had the enormous good fortune to be in the right place at the right time for forty years and, now that I have chosen a freelance life, I revel in the opportunities which it provides to make music with my many friends in the orchestral profession.

So music, 'the greatest good that man doth know, and all we have of Heaven below,' has helped me to win through with the help of my dear wife and family.

General Sir John Hackett
GCB CBE DSO MC

Sir John was born in Australia, the son of the late Sir John Winthrop Hackett KCMG LLD and was educated at Geelong Grammar School and New College, Oxford (Hon. Fellow 1972). Commissioned into his great-grandfather's regiment, the 8th KRI Hussars, in 1931, he served in Palestine in 1936, was seconded to the Trans-Jordan Frontier Force (1937–41), was wounded (with a MC) in Syria in 1941 and again in the Western Desert (with a DSO) in 1942. He raised and commanded the 4th Parachute Brigade in Egypt and Italy in 1943, and in 1944 was wounded at Arnhem.

From 1966–68 he was Commander-in-Chief of the British Army of the Rhine and Commander of the Northern Army Group in NATO, and for seven years after that Principal of King's College in the University of London.

A Freeman of the City of London, Sir John has been awarded honours by several universities and has written a number of books, including his controversial studies *The Third World War* and *The Untold Story*. He considers his best book to be *I Was a Stranger*, about Holland under German occupation in the last winter of the war.

We are privileged to print Sir John's own account of his Arnhem experience and the aftermath.

In late September of 1944 some 10,000 British airborne troops were landed in Holland to capture and hold the bridge across the Rhine at Arnhem. This would have let Allied troops into the heart of Germany and hastened the end of the war. German tanks met us, however, too strong for our light weapons and the best efforts of the relieving British forces to get up to us were unavailing. Only after one of the hardest battles of the whole war were some 2,500 eventually got back across the Rhine. I, having parachuted in, was not among them. Seriously wounded in the last days of the battle, I was left in a Dutch hospital, under German guard, where a captured Ambulance Unit of our own was at work.

A German and a British surgeon looked me over, with other wounded. 'We won't bother with that one,' said the German. 'I'll have a go,' said the Briton, who knew me. 'Wasting your time,' said the German. The British parachute surgeon, Lipmann Kessel, persisted and performed a surgical miracle. I lived. Lippy had already given me more than forty years of life (and of valued friendship) when he himself died earlier this year and was buried, at his request, in Holland near the graves of so many he had known and tended.

The fitness of a man fully prepared for airborne battle is so great that I was able, ten days after a major abdominal operation, to walk with Dutch help out of this German-held hospital and go into hiding. Then, for over four months, I was looked after in a Dutch household consisting of four middle-aged ladies and the son and daughter of one of them, hidden, nursed, well-fed in a time of near starvation, clothed, cherished and carefully watched over – all in a house in the Dutch township of Ede fifty yards or so from a German military police billet.

The de Nooij household was that of a Christian family. One sister who had studied to teach English possessed the Bible in the Authorized Version and, in the weeks that followed, I read it straight through. She also had, among other English books, a complete one-volume Shakespeare and I read every word of that too and, as with the Authorized Version, a good deal of it more than once.

This was a family living on a knife edge. The penalties for harbouring a British fugitive were extreme. It was a deeply Christian family, living in devout and loving kindness. It was also, therefore, a cheerful family. We were all, in our various ways, doing the best we could. The issue lay in other hands than our own. This taught me much that I would never afterwards forget, including what we mean in saying, 'Thy will be done'. When I was sufficiently restored (for my former strength had run out very soon) I said goodbye to my new family and with John, the son, rode off by bicycle through the winter snow, to cross the Rhine by night in secret and ride down to where a canoe waited on the River Waal to take me to the British lines, whence I could reach my family in England. I have been back to Ede many times, and members of the family in Holland have been to us here. Some are gone. Only one of the aunts survives, but relatives abound.

I wrote this story down and then kept the script for thirty years, to publish it in the end as a book. Of all that I learned in that friendly, courageous, Christian family in the Dutch township of Ede one thing above all else stood out. I had seen much bravery in battle. I now knew the unconquerable strength of the gentle. It need surprise no one to learn that my book was called *I Was A Stranger*.

Illtyd Harrington JP

Chairman of the Greater London Council in 1984–85, he was born in Wales in 1931, and educated at St Illtyd's R.C. School, Merthyr County School and Trinity College, Carmarthen. Entering local government in 1959, he joined the GLC in 1964 and became Alderman in 1970. Meanwhile, he rose to become Leader of the Labour Group of Westminster City Council in 1972. His service with the Council until 1986 was continuous, and ran concurrently with his many other interests, which include theatre administration and inland waterways. He is a Governor of Brunel University and in September 1986 was appointed Deputy Lieutenant of London.

He lists his recreations as laughing, singing, incredulity – and being a slave to local government, all of which are evidenced in the following reminiscence.

∞∞∞∞∞∞∞∞∞∞∞∞∞∞

When I was four years old I wanted to be the MP for my home town Merthyr Tydfil. At 40 years of age I failed to secure the Labour Party nomination. I was deeply sad. In 1973 I became Deputy Leader of the GLC but in 1980 I failed in my bid to become the Leader of my party and reluctantly continued as the Deputy Leader. These two events were not cataclysmic but they bruised me.

Yet the greatest crisis in my life, so far, began in late 1975 and was to dominate it until May 1977.

As Chairman of the Policy and Resource Committee of the GLC from 1973–77 I was in effect the 'Chancellor' of Greater London. I was the political head of a 5,000 million pound operation. I was proud of and thrilled by my job and its status. My life and work style was one of hyper-activity and I raced ahead.

Then I heard that my personal expense claims were being vetted by the District Auditor, the government scrutineer. I sent for this gentleman and the head of our financial department immediately. I had never completed the claims forms myself but accepted full responsibility for them. The meeting was a slightly menacing one and ended with me extremely worried, confused and paranoid. The District Auditor said I had over-claimed.

Political institutions breed rumour and intrigue and foolishly I had forgotten my enemies and the pettiness of certain people working near me. I decided not to convey my apprehension to anyone – thus foolishly exposing myself to a lonely and frightening period.

My reputation was at stake and I knew that some County Hall 'Iago' was out to destroy it.

I tried to continue my job but it became impossible to function efficiently. Then late one night I was told I was to be interviewed by two senior policemen from the Fraud Squad.

Those near me warned me to slow down but, as often happens to people in similar circumstances, I responded with a manic high. Then I decided to ask Lord Goodman for help. I rang him and he saw me immediately at his home in Portland Place. His great solid humanity brought me to my senses. I went home and cried but I felt stronger facing the destructive atmosphere in London's County Hall.

Soon after, I departed for Australia on behalf of the British Tourist Authority, of which I was a Board member, and on my return saw, on Lord Goodman's advice, Sir David Napley, the eminent London solicitor. He put me through a rigorous examination and left me feeling I had undergone major surgery without the benefit of anaesthetic.

My doubts, fears and lack of confidence grew more acute – sleep was rare and troubled. I was in an unbearable state of tension.

An interview was held at Sir David's office with the two policemen. Formal but scrupulously fair – I was hopeful that this would end the affair. Sir David did not share that view – he knew that there was only one place where my guilt or innocence could be determined.

In June 1976 Barbara Ward invited me to join Margaret Mead, the social anthropologist, and others in Vancouver to take part in the UN Habitat Conference. It was an honour which made me not a little proud. I crossed Canada twice in the week and on my last day went out to the idyllic side of Vancouver Island. A respite which proved to be the lull before the storm.

The next day I flew to New York, and received a telephone call from London that night telling me I was to be charged on ten counts of stealing about £144.77½p. The crisis had come.

My friends met me at Heathrow Airport and the next day I was fingerprinted and 'mug shot' and opened the midday edition of the *London Evening Standard*, which splashed my name and alleged offence.

It took an enormous effort to go into County Hall, but I knew it had to be done. In the next week or so my eyesight began to deteriorate dangerously and I became an outpatient at Moorfield's Eye Hospital where a doctor later told me I might lose my sight altogether. This could not be traced to any immediate source, but it seemed to me, in my debilitated state, almost a Biblical affliction.

Physically and mentally I was in bad shape and began a period of intense depression which necessitated long sessions with an eminent psychiatrist. The magistrates' court appearance was perfunctory but wounding. I was committed to stand my trial at the Old Bailey.

All of this involved long and tedious meetings with the

solicitors and hearing their suggestions for my QC. Their practicality and professionalism encouraged me. In deep self-pity I thought no one stood at my side.

My QC was George Shindler – now a judge. I went to two case conferences in the Temple and on the second occasion he told me my trial was to be postponed until mid-1977. I left that good, caring man heavy-hearted and suicidal. He had shaken my hand and said, 'I know you are going through the fire but it will end.' I wondered where and when.

Time hung heavily, but eventually in late May 1977 I stood in the dock in the famous No. 2 court and replied, 'Not Guilty,' ten times to the ten charges. Two friends came to the Old Bailey on that Monday morning, many others volunteered but I resisted this. On Friday lunchtime I was found 'Not Guilty' ten times. The long nightmare was over.

I left the dock with a spring in my step, a large group of friends had gathered outside the Old Bailey and they cheered me. Reporters plied me with celebratory champagne and the same *Evening Standard* which had first proclaimed my indictment pictured me rejoicing on their front page. We went off to the 'Gay Hussar', my favourite restaurant, for a thanksgiving lunch. My doctor sent a message and after lunch we drove off to his house deep in the Forest of Dean. The next day I walked in the forest, it was a bright May morning.

In that week friends proved friendship and acts of loyalty and love were effective and sustaining. Phone calls and letters came flooding in and a fund was launched to raise my legal costs of £3,000 – it was quickly oversubscribed.

As one of the organizers of the Queen's Jubilee celebrations in London, I went on the following Monday evening to the Royal Gala at Covent Garden. I had been deeply involved in all stages of the Jubilee and had made many new and unexpected friends and won approval for the GLC's support. Under the circumstances I was particularly thrilled to be there on such a glamorous night.

The Prime Minister, James Callaghan, greeted me warmly

and announced in an audible voice, 'it should never have gone to court'. Others eminent and unknown were equally kind – but the journey had been a lonely and depressing one.

It put me into a stress situation which nearly broke my personality and ruined my reputation. I was determined to fight and win. And, with the aid of my friends and a simple belief in my fellow men and women, I did.

My eyesight returned to normal, the curse was lifted.

I continued in my role as Deputy Leader of the GLC, was re-elected to the Council in 1981 with an enormous majority, and had the honour of being the Chairman of the Council from 1984–85. In due course, I was invited back to lunch with the judges at the Old Bailey. It was a modest but good meal and for me a particularly memorable one – and as always with judges, full of good jokes.

Rachael Heyhoe Flint MBE

Journalist, broadcaster, public speaker and sportswoman, Rachael Heyhoe Flint is best known as a member of the England Women's Cricket Team from 1960-83 and Captain for eleven years from 1966-77.

Educated at Wolverhampton High School for Girls and the Dartford College of Physical Education, where she gained a Diploma, she became Head of Physical Education at schools in Wolverhampton 1960-64. She was Coach to the US Field Hockey Association in 1964-65. Entering journalism in 1965 with the *Express* and *Star Wolverhampton*, she became the first TV woman Sports Reporter and from 1967 has been a *Daily Telegraph* Sports journalist. Among her many cricket achievements, she hit the first six in Women's Test cricket (Oval 1963) and scored the highest English test score in England and third highest in the world (179 runs for England v. Australia at the Oval in 1976).

Author of several books, now a public relations consultant and a busy after-dinner speaker, she is married to ex-Warwickshire cricketer Derrick Flint and has a family of four.

∞∞∞∞∞∞∞∞∞∞∞∞∞∞∞

My eleven-year reign as England captain ended abruptly on a Sunday afternoon in mid-July 1977. Fittingly, the sun didn't shine that day: it was damp, dark and drizzling, and as I walked across the cricket pitch in Halifax it seemed as if I was walking to the gallows: my stomach felt empty and I was strangely nervous.

The concluding trial match of the 1977 season, designed to finalize the selectors' plans for the forthcoming World Cup series in India, had been abandoned because of the rain, and now a message had been sent, summoning me across the ground to meet the selectors in the nearby tennis pavilion. Logically, I should have had no cause to fear. The previous summer's tour by Australia had been a success in every way and my personal form had seemed reasonable with an average of 87.5 and my career best, 179. I had been captain of my country for eleven years, during which we had not suffered a single Test match defeat.

But deep down, I knew exactly what to expect. In the past, being re-named as captain had only entailed my being taken aside for a brief moment in the dressing room prior to an official announcement – never anything so formal as a meeting with the selectors. Something, I knew instinctively, was wrong, and the sinking feeling in the pit of my stomach told me that this was to be the *coup de grace*. For the last twelve months the rapport which had always previously existed between the Women's Cricket Association and myself had visibly begun to crumble.

I remember that hundred-yard stroll so vividly, from leaving my friends in the hubbub of the dressing room, through being vaguely aware of mist clinging to the hills away to my left and an appalling smell wafting up from the nearby canal, to the moment when I arrived beneath the tennis pavilion balcony, face-to-face with the suitably solemn expressions...

Audrey Winterbottom, chairman of the selectors, was staring poker-faced over the balcony, and even at such a serious moment in my life I pictured her as a seasick traveller about to cast herself overboard. Kay Green, Sue Hilliam and Carole Evans, three of the other four selectors, sat silently apart. They looked blankly ahead as though they had been hypnotized! Audrey Disbury, the fifth selector, was not at that final match – I wondered if her absence was significant, for she had always been a very good friend of mine. Like the prisoner in the dock, I waited for sentence to be passed.

It seemed somehow intended that I should be standing at ground level, with the rain steadily soaking my unprotected head as I looked up at the chairman. Our opening exchange was ridiculously trite. 'Thank you for coming,' she said. 'It's a pleasure,' I replied.

Then Audrey Winterbottom drew breath, but still she couldn't bring herself to look me in the eye. Instead, staring vacantly over my head, she stiffly announced, 'I think I ought to tell you that you are not going to be named as captain for the touring team to India in December.'

However well one is prepared for any shock, it is never very easy to grasp when it actually happens, although in my mind I had rehearsed this part of the drama. I tried to be phlegmatic about it all, told myself 'that's it, it's over,' and prepared to turn and walk away without a word. Then I stopped and pulled myself together. After eleven years, I thought, at least I could ask for an explanation. I turned back to Audrey Winterbottom and politely asked, 'Can you tell me why?'

'It's a committee decision,' she replied formally.

'Is it anything to do with my playing form?' I ventured, knowing that logically it couldn't be.

'No.'

'In that case, is it anything I've done off the field?'

'I can't be specific. I cannot point to "A" or "B". It's a committee decision.'

And with that devastatingly frigid closing comment, the interview was obviously over. I saw no point in prolonging it, so muttered an absurd 'thank you' and turned for a walk back that seemed many times longer and more sad than any I had ever made after a dismissal in a match. My thoughts were racing – 'remember that stiff upper lip,' I said to myself!

My return was watched by all the players, many of whom had been personal friends over a number of years. They, too, had known that all was not well, and as they stood peering through the rain I almost felt an urge to shout to them. Instead I extended one arm out towards them and turned my thumb downwards.

Inside the pavilion a stunned silence reigned – but very different from the one which I had just left, a hundred yards away. I was greeted by expressions of shock and disbelief. Two of the younger girls burst into tears as I shook my head and announced, rather superfluously, 'Sorry, I'm not captain.'

Telling myself I must not break down, I walked on into the dressing room and began packing my cricket bag. I didn't dare look at anyone, but throughout the packing operation, different girls came up, tapping me on the back, telling me they were sorry and asking what they could do. Of course, the answer was nothing.

I then had a strong urge to go while I could. But I applied all the willpower I could muster and refused to run away before Rosemary Goodchild, the WCA chairman, arrived to make a formal announcement that Mary Pilling was to be the new captain of England. While I stared intently at the ground, an air of shock persisted around the dressing room. It seemed crazy, and very hurtful, and as I collected my kit and packed the car, I still didn't trust myself to speak.

Driving home across the Pennines on the M62 the words, 'You are no longer captain of England,' rang incessantly in my ears. I could easily have cried. I survived the journey by convincing myself that I had many compensations – a home, a husband and a son, to name just the most important three. When I told Derrick, my husband, what had happened, as he came out to help me unpack the car, he stared at me disbelievingly and said, 'That is utterly appalling.'

My whole philosophy in the sad situation was to carry on working and playing as though nothing had happened. In my situation you cannot fight the authorities and establishment; I just had to accept my fate with as much grace as possible and not be tempted into a public slanging match.

I think my attitude worked; within a year a completely new selection panel had been voted in and within eighteen months I was back in the fold of the WCA and playing for England once more.

Sir Immanuel Jakobovits the Chief Rabbi

Rabbi Sir Immanuel Jakobovits has been Chief Rabbi of the United Hebrew Congregations since 1967, prior to which he served for nine years as Rabbi of the Fifth Avenue Synagogue in New York.

He was educated at London University, where he graduated with a BA degree and later gained a PhD. Rabbi Jakobovits is a family man, having two sons and four daughters and is the author of books on Jewish law and medical ethics, in addition to contributions to learned and popular journals in America, England and Israel.

In the following narrative he recalls a major family crisis which occurred when he was Chief Rabbi of Ireland (1949–58). The account is an extract of a sermon on prayer delivered to his Congregation in New York on the New Year 1961.

~~~~~~~~~~~~~~~~~~~~~~~

My greatest personal crisis happened in Ireland, when I was faced with the almost certain death of my baby daughter. Dehydrated and emaciated to her little bones, she was rushed to hospital in a pitiful state and the doctors' hopes faded, as she would not respond to treatment.

At the height of the crisis my friends joined in a heartrending plea for mercy by reciting the Book of Psalms together at the end of our morning prayer service. Snatched from the Angel of Death by prayer, my baby made a miraculous recovery and today is the happy mother of four children.

I am by training and temperament too much of a rationalist to be usually given to mystic beliefs, but during my ten years in Ireland there were two other occasions – and only two – when we publicly recited the Book of Psalms for desperately ill patients. In both cases our prayers were answered.

The first time it was an old man, devout and beloved by the community. He was sinking fast, and the doctors had given up all hope for his recovery. One morning, in our despair, we called the congregation together and implored God in readings from the Psalms to spare this wonderful man's life. From that very day the tide began to turn; he rallied and recovered miraculously.

On the next occasion it concerned a young girl, a pupil of our religious classes. She had been struck by a severe attack of polio. Placed in an oxygen tent, her life ebbed visibly. The doctors told the grief-stricken parents to be prepared for the worst. Once more the congregation gathered to say the Book of Psalms. Defying the medical prognosis, she suddenly regained her strength and she was back at our school a few months later.

True prayer enlists the heart more than the brain; even the illiterate can pray with the deepest devotion. The story is told of a simple peasant who appeared before the founder of Chasidism soon after the conclusion of Yom Kippur grief-stricken that he could not join the congregation in prayer on the holy day. In weeping tones he told the great Rebbe that, as he was about to close his little store and to go on his way on the eve of Yom Kippur, he was held up by some officials who engaged him until nightfall, forcing him to spend the holy day in his village where there were no facilities for a religious service. He had no prayer book, nor could he read anything except the letters of the alphabet. Thus he sat all day broken-hearted going over the Hebrew alphabet and hoping that God would order his disjointed letters into prayers. How could he now atone for his absence from the synagogue on Yom Kippur? After listening to this tale of woe, the founder of Chasidism placed his hands on the head of his petitioner and exclaimed, 'For the past ten years no prayer as beautiful and pure as yours has ascended to Heaven.'

This, then, is the road of prayer. It strengthens us to bear our burdens and to persevere in adversity. In the touching words of the famed Yiddish writer Peretz, 'Prayer sometimes dulls the hunger of the pauper, like a mother's finger thrust into the mouth of her starving baby.'

Miriam Karlin

The daughter of Harry Samuels, a barrister, Miriam Karlin was born in London and trained for the theatre at RADA. Her career spans the whole of the post-war period and she has appeared in every branch of entertainment except, as she says, ballet and the circus.

After her stage debut in 1947 she rapidly came to the fore in the theatre, radio and TV. Readers will remember her successes in *Variety Bandbox* (radio series with Peter Sellers), *The Rag Trade* (TV series), *Fiddler on the Roof* (Her Majesty's Theatre in 1967, in which she starred opposite Topol), her one-woman show *Liselotte* which toured, after its London run, at the Edinburgh Festival, in Vienna and in Australia.

From 1981-83 she played with the Royal Shakespeare Company, during which period they opened the Barbican Arts Centre, and followed this with her tour of *84 Charing Cross Road*, which won her the *Manchester Evening News* Award. After her success in *Torch Song Trilogy* in 1986 she rejoined the RSC for a further season.

A sufferer from back pains for many years and having to cope with a continuous work programme, she became a victim of submission to prescribed tranquillizers and here she tells of her battle to overcome the addiction and to regain mastery of her emotions.

~~~~~~~~~~~~~~~~~~~~~~~~

The whole horror story started when, after years of constant suffering from back pains, I went into hospital for an operation which was to make me a new woman, or so I was assured. Now, over the years I had been taking a minimal dose of a tranquillizer – four mg per day – to enable me to damp down the pain and carry on my profession, and I thought the period of hospitalization would provide just the opportunity to be weaned off it. Unfortunately the surgeon thought otherwise; he recommended increasing the dose to fifteen mg, which initially staggered me.

However, such are the workings of the mind that while the logical side of me felt it was a retrograde step, the other – the insecure and weaker side – was secretly delighted. I was now to take a comforting daily dose legitimately and on medical recommendation. The doctors also gave me massive doses of antidepressants but these I managed to discard two months after leaving hospital. Not so, however, the tranquillizers, for the simple reason that I had become hopelessly hooked on the increased dose within a matter of weeks.

In my heart I knew this was wrong and for that reason I never talked to anyone about it. What was more, the surgeon had arranged for me to wear a steel corset after the operation and here was I, months later, high-kicking in a musical in a steel corset – little wonder I needed the drugs!

The operation had been a total disaster. The pain was no less and I had become a hopeless drug addict. In 1985 I was strongly advised to take steps to eradicate the drug dependency, which by now was reckoned to be encouraging my pain rather than alleviating it. I was then about to open in *Torch Song Trilogy* at the Albery Theatre, so it was decided that I should postpone the necessary treatment until the end of the run, which I did.

Those who have become dependent on medication will know the form. I had by now cut down my daily dose from fifteen mg to ten mg, but I would not dare to go to the theatre without my supply. I have even returned home when half way there, on discovering I had left my pills behind.

So it was that, at the end of the run of the play, I arranged to go into the Charter Clinic in Chelsea for a stay of ten days. And even then my own impetuosity – a fault which has dogged me all my life – led me into another ghastly experience. There were a few days before I was due to go into the clinic, so I decided, off my own bat, to stop taking my drugs immediately and completely! The result was appalling. After three days my eyes stood out on stalks and I looked revolting. I rushed off to my doctor, who immediately ordered me to resume a small dose and to leave my cure to the clinic.

I arrived there taking five mg per day and they systematically reduced it by one mg each day. This resulted in a corresponding reduction in my sleep and after the first five days I was having no sleep at all.

The process of 'detoxification', as it is called, was most interesting, despite the accompanying trauma. The experience was uplifting. I was there among all kinds of sufferers – alcoholics, heroin addicts, manic depressives, agoraphobics – and one got involved in daily group therapy, which I found fascinating. I couldn't wait to get to the sessions. Funnily enough, it was just like a first rehearsal of a new play, when all the cast sit around and discuss the characters very intimately and in detail.

So there I was, after five days – off the drugs, not sleeping – and I did not sleep for seven or eight days after that. But I had such an enormous store of energy that I got by. However, you do not go through that kind of experience without damaging yourself, and the answer is to avoid becoming dependent in the first place. Withdrawal and readjustment from tranquillizers can be more difficult than from heroin. In the case of the hard drugs you can be given milder alternatives as an intermediate help during withdrawal. What is more, in those cases addiction and deterioration are usually fairly rapid, whereas with prescribed relaxants and the like you have to cope with a long, gradual build-up, without the help of milder alternatives during withdrawal. I was given nothing, except a lot of talk and a lot of exercise.

Having said that, I must say that the treatment I had in the clinic was wonderful and I would thoroughly recommend it to anybody faced with a similar problem. Let's face it – everybody who is prescribed tranquillizers has, at some stage, to come off them, or remain for the rest of their life in less than full control of themselves. Looking back over my own six years of total addiction to fifteen mg per day I think of myself as being wrapped in a kind of mental clingfilm – my brain, my heart, all my emotions. There was no depth in any of my feelings or reactions; everything was shallow. Oddly enough, I was able to cope with acting and the emotions involved in playing a part. Maybe, being Jewish, I am naturally able to display emotion more readily than some.

And now, as I write, I am about to go into a new play. How am I to cope? It will be the first time for years that I have faced a first night without any 'props'. However, I am determined after all I have gone through, not to throw it all out of the window and I know I shall win through.

Finally, I have a first-class incentive. I decided, after my cure, to campaign on behalf of those who need similar help and this I have now started to organize. It is very important, especially for young people, to realize that they must not allow themselves to submit permanently to mentally harmful medication. You must be your own master and break out of the clingfilm.

Colonel Ronald Kaulback OBE

After leaving Cambridge with a taste for zoology and exploration, Ronald Kaulback accompanied an expedition through Assam and Eastern Tibet with the late Kingdon Ward, returning to Tibet two years later looking for the source of the Salween River. This was followed by eighteen months in Upper Burma hunting and collecting zoological specimens for the British Museum.

He spent the early part of the Second World War as Chief Instructor at the Small Arms School, later returning to Burma with his own independent command.

As a successful postwar hotelier for thirty years on the west coast of Ireland, he was no less unconventional and attracted the kind of guest who valued eccentricity, coupled with excellent cuisine and a sensitive cellar.

Now in retirement, he is busy learning Russian.

I lost a leg the other day – eleven months ago, to be exact. The accident happened as I was about to get into bed. I went to the window to draw back the curtains, slipped on something, fell and broke my thigh. It was as simple as that. In hospital they asked me my age (I was seventy-six) and put me in traction, flat on my back with my leg in a kind of cradle, and a weight over a pulley keeping the leg in tension; and so I stayed for twelve weeks, waiting for the bone to set. It would take all that time, I was told, because old bones take longer to heal than young ones; but, even after the three months were up, there was still no sign of the bone knitting. So, still not giving up hope of saving the leg, the surgeons operated twice in the next month, each time without success, and after that I told them we had better cut our losses and have the thing off. It appears that they were going to tell me the same thing, but I got in first, which pleased me.

The reason I have gone into such detail here is because the four months I had to wait before matters came to a head meant that I had had plenty of time to come to terms with the problem. I might so easily have had an entirely different sort of accident (been run over by a bus, perhaps), and woken up to be told that my leg had had to be taken off. It would have been an appalling shock to me: but, as things were, I had no sort of shock at all; and, in fact, when I came to after the operation, I felt nothing but a great relief that all that business was now over. At last I was without pain – apart from the 'phantom pains' which smote me pretty often in the missing leg, and which get fewer and fewer as time goes on. Very odd they are too, because I know exactly where each pain is, and could point a finger at the very spot (big toe, or knee or whatever), and yet there's no real leg there at all.

As though determined to follow, at all costs, the old saying that whatever one does should be done thoroughly or not at all, the surgeons made a real job of my leg and took it off completely, hip joint and all. What they left is just a small, plump and (to me, at least) rather endearing little stump, which, after a while, I found I could waggle at will in all directions, much to my surprise and satisfaction. The experts had been a little gloomy about my chances of being able to have any sort of artificial leg on so small a stump; but this power of waggling made them think again and they became quite optimistic. For the last seven weeks I have had a fine, upstanding, if rather primitive leg, which not only does a lot for my appearance (even at my advanced age that is quite important!), but means that I can stand, without crutches, and do things like cooking or odd jobs, WITH BOTH HANDS FREE. And, too, I can get around with it a good deal better than I ever could when there was just a stump.

But to go back to those hospital days and the first few weeks after I left: when word spread around that Kaulback was legless, letters began to arrive in considerable numbers, full of sympathy and friendship and all of them warming to my heart. Bless all those letter-writers, and those, too, who came to see me in hospital for their generous kindness. None the less, it did strike me after a time that I was receiving all this sympathy very much under false pretences, and that, if I wasn't careful, I might even sink into a slough of self-pity. What was there really for people to sympathize about? I am already comfortably over the three score and ten and, on the whole, I have had a lovely life. Not much money – a lack which has not worried me greatly – but all the things which matter so much more than that. I have had them all, things such as good health, friends (as opposed to acquaintances), the love of the women I have loved; and so very much more. I have been able to lead the active life I always wanted, and up till now I have never had anything much more than a scratch on me. I no longer yearn to play physical games or engage in tough sports; I would far rather watch others show their skills; and so, if I have to do without a leg, this is the very time to do without it. Now that I can get about quite easily (and only a little more slowly than before) what on earth have I got to complain about?

However strange it may seem, now that the actual business of losing it is over and done with, this being without a leg is interesting and quite fun. There are so many little difficulties to sort out that there is hardly a dull moment. How to wash myself in the bath is still one of them. I like plenty of water in the bath, but when I lift up my leg to get busy on that, unless I hang on to the sides of the bath like a limpet I instantly spin round and dunk myself. Even if I hang on with only one hand, it is hard to control the soap with just the other. And what about chest and stomach? To get those portions of the anatomy above water level it is necessay to push with both hands on the bottom of the bath – so then what? It's no use trying to stand up on my one leg either, and wash like that. It's not possible, for me at any rate. But there – Archimedes got his best ideas in the bath, and I too will solve this problem in time. Meanwhile there are many others to occupy me pleasantly.

I have no complaints at all. Life is certainly different from what it was, but it is interesting and very satisfying and, above all, I don't feel a cripple.

Esmond Knight

Esmond Knight who died at the age of eighty in February 1987, was a veteran English actor. After fifteen years on the English stage, he joined the RNVR in 1940 to serve in World War II. Blinded while in action in 1941, he refused to accept the permanence of his disability and rejected the opinion of the specialists. He tells how he regained his sight and was able to resume his theatrical career, which flourished for forty years.

Esmond Knight held the distinction of being the only British naval officer to be blinded in action and the only man from St Dunstan's, the famous home for blind ex-servicemen, known to have recovered his sight.

∞∞∞∞∞∞∞∞∞∞∞∞

They all laughed when I told them I had decided to have a cataract operation by a doctor who was off the Medical Register. They laughed because the best 'eye' men in London had told me I would never see again and that I must make up my mind to being blind for the rest of my life. I was an officer in the Royal Naval Volunteer Reserve, having joined up in 1940, and had lost my sight in 1941, when a fifteen-inch shell from the *Bismarck* had come through the bridge of HMS *Prince of Wales* killing a large proportion of its personnel, treating me to a dose of molten bits in the chest and face. Only moments before, *Hood*, the pride of the Fleet, had been blown up. We were badly mauled and limped back to Iceland, running perilously low in oil.

I was sent to the 30th General Hospital in Reykjavik where my left eye was excised and my remaining one, being full of blood, was sightless. It was hoped this would clear but it didn't and, having spent all summer in that barren, fish-manured island, I was sent back to England, as they said they could do nothing more for me. Arriving at Gourock, on the Clyde, the medical officer informed me that I was to be sent straight away to St Dunstan's, at that time situated in the Long Mynd Hotel at Church Stretton in Shropshire. This piece of news was effectively the confirmation of my fate; I had been chucked out of the Navy and was officially designated as a blind man, who would inevitably have to spend the rest of his life in darkness.

This I found quite unacceptable. Of course, I had to submit to the harsh rules and regulations of St Dunstan's and to adjust myself to the spurious bonhomie that seemed to have settled on the newly blinded who, apart from the devoted nursing staff, were the only inhabitants. I reluctantly applied myself to the study of Braille and touch-typing, but all this I bitterly resented as it was tantamount to an admission and acceptance of permanent blindness. I remained there for six months.

Back in London I resolved not to take the situation lying down and so I went the rounds of the best ophthalmic surgeons, including the consultant to His Majesty the King. They were all of the same opinion – nothing could be done for me and I must make the most of my situation. What, then, was to be my future? Here was I, a trained actor with over fifteen years experience in the theatre, and if I had no future in my profession what was to become of me? The prospect was bleak indeed.

Then I had a great stroke of luck. My old friend, the film producer Michael Powell, invited me to play a part in a new film entitled *The Silver Fleet* and starring Ralph Richardson and Googie Withers. It was about submarines being built in Holland during the war and I was cast as a rather unpleasant Nazi interrogation officer. By careful preparation and practice in rehearsal I was able to portray this sighted character and, perhaps due to my professional experience, my blindness was not evident, as the notices were quite good. This was a start, but I wondered how many producers would be willing to follow Michael Powell's lead and employ me now? Time, indeed, showed the stark reality and I had to admit to myself that, despite a success in *The Silver Fleet*, I was back at square one again, with little or no prospects.

And then came the miracle – the miracle of my sight being restored by a surgeon who had been struck off the Medical Register. Dr Vincent Nesfield had been found guilty of unorthodox practice in that he habitually operated in all departments of surgery when he was meant to be an eye specialist. Doc Nesfield, who was introduced to me by my brother, was a paradox of a character – a revolutionary who spurned the restrictions of the official bodies and a reactionary who had no time for newfangled equipment. He would not use an ophthalmoscope and at my first meeting with him he shone an old-fashioned bull's-eye torch into my eye. Nevertheless, he announced that if he could not guarantee me useful sight he could predict that I would, at least, achieve a good perception of light if I allowed him to treat me.

In March 1943 he operated on my eye, removing the cataract, and four months later gave me a needling and a course of his home-made injections. These were a concoction of unbelievable ingredients, but they worked. It was while at his nursing home on the edge of Romney Marsh that the miracle took place. I awoke one morning to find that I could distinguish the square outline of the window frame. Later that day I was given a flower in the garden. I held it up to my eye. 'Yellow, isn't it?' I asked nervously. I was holding a humble dandelion, but to me, in that moment, it was the most wonderful of flowers. From that day my sight steadily improved and I had the unforgettable experience of recognising again familiar sights like advertising posters 'Guinness', 'The Bisto Kids', 'Players Please'.

At first I had difficulty in trusting this new situation. During my two years of total blindness I had frequently experienced a very unpleasant nightmare. In my dream I had regained my sight and would run to the window, to look out over miles of country. Then suddenly I would awake, to realize it was not true and that I was still in a world of darkness. Now the dream was the reality, and as my sight improved daily I overcame my fear and began to realize my new potential.

Joy was added to joy when I had a telephone call from Laurence Olivier. He had been to see his good friend Ralph Richardson in *The Silver Fleet* and as a result, was offering me the part of Fluellen in his great epic film, *Henry the Fifth*, which he was then casting. It must be remembered that, at that time, suitable actors were hard to find, and I, invalided out of the forces, was to hand and available. This, for me, was the stepping stone – the vital opportunity I needed, now that I could see again. In 1948 Anthony Quayle invited me to join the Royal Shakespeare Company at Stratford-upon-Avon and such was my restored sight – and restored confidence – that I bicycled, on my own, all over the Cotswolds. Indeed, I was to enjoy a further twenty-five years of normal sight and continuous work in the theatre, films and television, after having known the severe limitation of total blindness. At one stage, on location, I actually drove a car through the centre of Rome, an exploit hazardous enough even to the experienced motorist.

If I may add a postscript, it is to say that some years ago my sight began to fade through secondary glaucoma and today I can see nothing. Nevertheless I am still acting and enjoying life; as I write I am just off to Cairo to play an ageing eccentric in a BBC saga called *The Fortunes of War*. I can only say to those who are assailed by misfortune – never give up.

Peter Macann

Peter Macann, the television presenter of BBC's *Tomorrow's World* was born in Teheran in 1944 and came to England at the age of three. He and his elder brother were both Cathedral Choristers at Winchester, earning their living, as Peter says, from the age of eight. He went on to Tonbridge School and at seventeen joined the Central School of Speech and Drama. After several years in repertory and a short spell on the London stage, he accepted an offer to present a TV programme and has been engaged in television ever since.

He is married and has one son and twin daughters.

Peter Macann was one of the crew of the ill-fated *Atlantic Challenger* speedboat crossing in 1985 and of the successful follow-up in 1986.

It was quite by coincidence that I became involved in the first *Atlantic Challenger* crossing. The first I knew of the operation was when we were sent down by the BBC to the shipyard at Littlehampton where the hull of the catamaran was being built, to do a story for *Tomorrow's World* on the technology of a craft being specially designed to cross the Atlantic at a record-breaking speed. That was in November 1984.

It was to be an impressive boat, fifty-seven feet in length and powered by two 2,000 h.p. engines and I was immediately struck by the enthusiasm of everybody working on it. It was something never attempted before; they were all obsessed by it and before the day was out I, too, had caught the fever.

I have always been a keen sailor, added to which I had trained as a diver, had done an army survival course on Dartmoor and an astronaut training course at Houston and, in my keenness to be invited to join the crew, I unashamedly paraded these assets before Ted Tolman, who was to be the skipper – and, in fact, was the originator of the whole idea. A man of few words, Ted was noncommittal at the time, but a few days later I received an invitation to attend his doctor for a medical. The BBC then agreed that I should go and should film the voyage on their behalf.

Once the boat was launched we carried out trials off the English coast, based on the Hamble river, while the fitting out was being completed at Ted Tolman's yard. It was then driven round to Liverpool, from where it was to be taken by container boat across to New York. We all flew over to New York, picked up the boat and then began what we came to know as 'the waiting game'. Day after day, week after week, we waited for the right weather, occupying the time with tests of the equipment, tuning the propellers, and general training. With any boat there is always plenty to occupy the crew, and with a powerboat there are extra factors due to the necessity to plane at speed, involving fine adjustments.

At the last moment, when all was right for the start, including the Atlantic weather, there was a hitch involving our best set of propellers and we actually set off on the crossing using our second-best set and being led up Long Island Sound by a local boat in thick fog.

The first part of the journey was fair, but after the first night we ran into a thunderstorm, which cut all our communications and caused a temporary panic. But the sea was reasonably calm most of the time and in a thirty-foot sailing boat, cruising at twelve knots, life would have been comfortable. However, a thirty-ton catamaran speeding along at fifty knots leaps into the air over each wave top and a couple of seconds later comes plummetting down again with a gigantic smack – and this precludes anything like sleep or serious relaxation. However, I was filming as well as taking my turn at driving, so had little time to notice fatigue. I must admit there were times when I felt convinced the boat could not survive indefinitely. Being lifted up and flung down again every few seconds it must be only a matter of time. If you had to get from one part of the boat to another it could take twenty minutes. With every step you took you might leave the ground and become totally weightless as the whole boat took off into the air. And even as you thought, 'Here we go again!' you would come crashing down, probably landing on somebody's lap as they were trying to get some rest. My own difficulties in handling and servicing my cameras in these conditions were indescribable, but sanity was saved by everyone falling about with laughter.

I was driving when things started to happen. I was convinced we already had a list to starboard. We pumped out the starboard hull and sure enough, the boat seemed to right itself. It was not long, however, before the engineer reported that the starboard hull had actually split. That was the first really bad moment. We knew there was nothing we could do to prevent the inevitable happening, but we had agreed in advance that in an emergency we must always keep going, at all costs. To stop would mean we could never get up on the plane again and we would be trapped, wallowing around with no further hope. So we had this bizarre situation, whereby we were still pressing ahead at forty knots with half a hull flapping off, stretching everything to maintain maximum speed while the needles slowly but steadily dropped back and back. Eventually we lost traction and the water started to pour in. I think the most frightening moment for me, after the initial shock, was when we all had to get into our survival suits. I knew from my diving days that to get, or to fall, into the water with the suit imperfectly adjusted and fastened can be fatal. The water seeps in and drags you down. In this case we had a very limited time, the suits were clumsy and difficult to get into and they zipped up diagonally across the back! People were desperately trying to scramble into their suits and I knew that if the boat sank suddenly, some of us would not survive.

Once all suits were properly secured it was back to filming for me. This was a cameraman's dream – a sinking ship and an exclusive! I was all organised and programmed for the eventuality. I had my 'panic bag' of basic equipment, all ready in case of abandoning ship. But then my emergency camera refused to work. It was a bizarre moment. One hull deep in the water, everybody getting into the life rafts and myself perched on the floating deck feverishly changing batteries. But the camera would not work and I jumped into the raft with the others, reduced to talking into a tape recorder.

We were in two dinghies strapped together, and the nine of us turned to watch the death throes of the *Challenger*. We had drifted away from the boat and as we watched we saw the bow slowly rise at first, until the whole boat seemed to expire and slide away, with an audible hiss. It was an emotional moment – we all had a deep feeling of bereavement.

Our timely and efficient rescue by a Geest banana boat and our subsequent homecoming were widely publicized and we were reckoned fortunate to have survived the incident.

However, for me the crux of the matter came when I was invited to take part in the follow-up attempt with a new boat, the next year. This invitation involved me in a very major decision. All of us who crewed the first ill-fated attempt had invested heavily in terms of personal commitment and the job had not been finished. The urge to accept and to contribute to the successful completion of the operation was a natural and proper one. On the other hand, my wife was carrying our twin babies and I had no right to gamble with my life at that time. Fortunately for me, she was entirely supportive and understanding and it was her active encouragement which resulted in my joining the crew again.

The second *Atlantic Challenger* completed the course in record-breaking time in June 1986. We had won through.

Robert Maxwell MC

Robert Maxwell is Chairman of Mirror Group Newspapers Ltd., Founder and Publisher of Pergamon Press, Chairman of BPCC and a director of Central Television. He has also produced and co-produced a number of films.

Born in Czechoslovakia, he served in the British Army during the 1939–45 war, being awarded the Military Cross, and in the German Section of the Foreign Office until 1947. He was Labour Member of Parliament for Buckingham (1964–70) and Chairman of the Labour National Fundraising Foundation throughout the sixties.

Robert Maxwell has been honoured with an Hon. D.Sc of the Polytechnic Institute of New York (1985), and Hon. D.Sc of Moscow State University, the Royal Swedish Order of Polar Star (Officer 1st Class) and the Bulgarian People's Republic Order Stara Planina (1st Class).

His personal interest in fund-raising for charity and in particular for children, is well known.

~~~~~~~~~~~~~~~~~~~

Like millions of others I will never forget the horrors of the last war: torture; starvation; medical experiments; the gas chamber; the firing squad; the population of a village locked in a synagogue and burned alive. The stench of death in Hitler's Third Reich knew no limits. They destroyed families across the lands of earth. I was fifteen when they destroyed mine.

My mother, my brother and my five sisters had all been

rounded up and taken to Auschwitz. Behind the barbed wire of that evil and Godforsaken place they were humiliated, degraded and cruelly punished for their beliefs.

Then they were killed.

The massacre of my loved ones devastated me. I was consumed by grief and anger. But I also knew that my life now had a vital purpose. To avenge, fight for a free world, and win through.

The brave men and women of the Resistance were risking their lives hourly to sabotage the Hitler machine, set up escape routes and provide vital information for the Allies. So I told a white lie, said I was eighteen, and joined the Czech freedom fighters. On each and every mission the memory of my family and what the Nazis had done to them was imprinted on my mind.

Danger was ever present, culminating in my being arrested by Hungarian Border guards. Czechoslovakia was a protectorate of Hitler's Reich so any Czech who fought against Germany faced the death sentence. My arrest was my appointment with the firing squad. Luckily for me, however, my guards were blunderers and I managed to escape.

Resistance contacts organized a safe passage out of the country. I took part in the Battle of France in the summer of 1940, when France was defeated. I had a choice of destination, the United States which weren't as yet in the war, or Britain, whose people were laying their lives on the line in freedom's name. I chose Britain, and arrived at Liverpool in September 1940 with a rifle in my hand. I wanted to fight in the British Army, signed up, and spent four years working and training.

At the battle of Normandy I was commissioned in the field and was in the thick of the bloodiest fighting till the end.

Because, legally, I was a national in occupied Czechoslovakia I risked being summarily executed by the German army if captured, so the British Army advised me to change my name. The Army gave me the name of Leslie Jones as my family name of Jan Lodvik Hick was obviously Czech. Then I was given the name of du Maurier.

94 *Winning Through*

During the battle of Normandy I was involved in an action which was reported over the radio by the great war correspondent, Chester Willmot. He announced my name, du Maurier, so another name change was inevitable. My senior officer gave me the identity I have kept ever since – Robert Maxwell.

During the battle on the River Ruhr on the Dutch–German border in an offensive to capture the industrial heartland of Germany, I was engaged in beating off the German counter attack which resulted in Field Marshal Montgomery decorating me with the immediate award of the Military Cross. And it was for ignoring an order to retreat!

We were under heavy fire when the order went out to retreat. But I could not obey. For the sake of my brave comrades. For the sake of my beloved family.

Monty's award was for heroism in the face of enemy action and I still cherish it today. That MC is my family's MC.

Recently I was asked to write about the things I wish I'd known at eighteen. One is that I had not been parted from my parents so early and had been able to get to know them better. I did not know when I left Czechoslovakia that I would never see them again. My father had survived through much of the war but was shot by Germans shortly before the end of hostilities. That is a grief that can never be wiped out. I still miss my parents, sisters and brother desperately.

But their loss and the experience of war helped prepare me for the many difficulties I was to encounter along life's highway: to be brave; to be strong; to be determined; to win through.

Stirling Moss OBE

Born in 1929 and educated at Haileybury and Imperial Service College, he became a professional motor racing driver and was British National Champion ten times between 1950 and 1961. He won the Tourist Trophy seven times, the *Coupe des Alpes* three times and had three consecutive wins in the Alpine Gold Cup. He is also the only Englishman to win the Italian *Mille Miglia* (1955). Stirling Moss competed in no less than 494 races, rallies, sprints, land speed records and endurance runs and won 222 of these.

He has written ten books on various aspects of the motor racing world and is now President of thirty-six motoring clubs. In the following article he tells of the serious crash in 1962, which resulted in his retirement from the profession and how he rebuilt his life.

∞∞∞∞∞∞∞∞∞∞∞∞∞∞∞

I was a professional motor racing driver. When I left school I went into the hotel trade for a short period, during which I did some motor racing as an amateur. I became a professional when I was nineteen and remained one until I was thirty-two, when a serious crash forced me out of racing for good. It took about forty minutes to cut me out of the car. That was on Easter Monday, 1962 at Goodwood.

I was unconscious for a month and paralyzed for six months. For some time after I came round I did not realize the seriousness of my injuries and the doctors did not immediately tell me, knowing how some people would be disturbed to be told they were paralyzed. However, my best friend, who visited me regularly, knew my character and told me the true facts – that I was paralyzed all down the left side of my body. As soon as I knew, I realized it was a problem and one that I must, and would, overcome. I firmly believe that nearly anything you really want to do you *can* do if you really get down to it – and I am a bit cussed as well. Two years before, I had broken my back and both my legs and I was driving again after two months. And now, as a lay person, I could not accept that because you had a bang on the head it was going to tell one side of you not to work. After all, whose head is it? Who's in charge? When the mechanics were explained to me I had to begin to learn to move, bit by bit; first my fingers, then my head, my arm and gradually progress to full use again, learning eventually to lift things. I must say that it needed a tremendous mental effort as well as a physical one.

After six months I was allowed to leave hospital, to recuperate in the Bahamas. Out there it was quiet, the weather was kind, there were few people and cars about and I was able to try out my driving and to start walking and moving around. The Press were, by then, putting pressure on me, asking when I would be going back to racing and I saw no reason at first why I should not soon be back.

But about a year after the accident I went down to Goodwood to try myself out in a racing car. I went round the circuit and my time was quite good, but I realized that my concentration had gone and my intuitive feeling for the delicate and essential decisions was no longer present. I decided it would not do for me to try to return to professional racing and I decided I must retire.

So, I had to make a living. I was the highest paid racing driver in the year that I crashed, but money then was very little, relative to what can be earned today and I needed a source of income.

I had no qualifications. My father was a dentist and the

original idea was for me to become a dentist and take over his practices, which I could not do as I could not pass my exams to get into hospital and study for my MB. So I found myself, at the age of thirty-two, with no commercial background other than something which was not really saleable, faced with the problem of what I was going to do. With most sporting occupations, should you be a tennis or golf player for instance, you can usually become a pro and teach, but with motor racing you cannot, at least not to any extent. I do give instruction now and again, but it is not something on which you can base a career.

I looked around to see what one could do without being brainy and without experience. I had a little knowledge of the hotel trade or I could become an estate agent or a politician. You don't need any training for politics – in fact it is a disadvantage. But, I thought, politics is not for me, and in any case I am not a comedian, so it's not in my line. I therefore decided to go into public relations and also, with the little money I had made, into property in a small way. I bought a small amount of property from my father – some of his surgeries had upstairs living accommodation – and I did conversions for letting. I am, fortunately, a handyman and I was able to take a part in the work. On occasion, I have personally installed central heating, for instance, and greatly enjoyed it.

As I progressed, I formed my own design company, took on people to work for me and gradually got off the ground. However, apart from providing a basic income I have never felt that being a landlord was the be-all and end-all, so I developed the public relations aspect and my time is now devoted, with great satisfaction, to engaging in promotions, writing for magazines, lecturing and public speaking. I do not claim credit for these attributes. I had no qualifications, but they all stem from having made my name in motor racing. I think my story shows that there is always hope for the future if you refuse to accept defeat.

Countess Mountbatten of Burma CD JP DL

Daughter of Admiral-of-the-Fleet Earl Mountbatten of Burma, she succeeded her father in 1979 after his tragic assassination by the IRA. Married to Lord Brabourne and the mother of seven children, Lady Mountbatten of Burma is Vice Lord-Lieutenant of the County of Kent and a magistrate. She has devoted her life to innumerable good causes, among them the Red Cross, the NSPCC, the Save The Children Fund, the SOS Children's Villages, SSAFA and the Shaftesbury Society.

In her reaction to the events of 1979 and her subsequent coming to terms with her personal and family tragedy, she has shown an indomitable spirit and we thank her for allowing us to reprint her narrative.

Since it was the last week of our annual holidays, if the weather had turned bad we would probably not have gone out. The boat engine wasn't reliable and my father didn't want to risk things for the children.

We were in a happy holiday mood. Those who wanted to go out in the boat were getting ready, but mercifully our twins were the only children who wanted to come out with us. The group consisted of Doreen, Lady Brabourne, my mother-in-law; my father; my husband; the fourteen-year-old twins

Nicholas and Timothy, Paul Maxwell and myself. Paul was running the boat for us that year.

It was the most beautiful day, hot and sunny and breathless. We sailed for about five or ten minutes from the harbour on our way to pick up the lobster pots, and to have a few hours out. The last thing I remember my mother-in-law saying was, 'Isn't it a beautiful day!' At that moment the bomb went off.

I can't remember being blown out of the boat, but I can remember being in the water and feeling that I was going round and round. I remember hearing voices and I was aware that they were agitated. They were fishing us out of the water. Practically nothing was left of the boat, just bits of matchwood. Nicholas died in the blast and went down with the boat. Paul Maxwell was picked up dead. My other twin, Timothy, who was sitting on the roof, was blown off into the sea. He was picked up later doing a kind of dog paddle. My father was lifted out of the water by a young couple who were out fishing. He died instantly, thank God.

When my mother-in-law was picked up she wasn't very badly hurt. If she hadn't been 83 she might have survived. She died mostly of shock the next morning.

My husband had very badly injured legs, one so bad they thought he would lose it, but luckily he didn't. He suddenly found himself lying on me on the bottom of the boat, and he thought I was dead. I must have looked awful. My face was totally lacerated. I later had 120 stitches in it, even in my eyeballs.

We were in hospital in Sligo for three weeks. The people in the Sligo hospital were wonderful and nothing was too much trouble. I had a badly broken leg, my eardrums were gone and I am still slightly deaf. We went home with a nurse, in wheelchairs and then we were months on crutches.

I cried every day for perhaps six months to a year and intermittently for the next year. I can still cry over it very easily, after six years.

I believe strongly in hope. If you lose hope, you lose all

desire to live. What brought me through was the realization that I was still alive and that I had better get on with it, and that the family still needed me, and that I couldn't go round moping miserably because it wasn't fair on them.

My advice to those who have been bereaved or injured would be to talk about it, if possible. It's enormously helpful not to shut it in. If they have members of their family or a good friend who is able to listen, it is extremely important to talk. Also, you've got to accept the situation. There's no point in fighting against it, no point in saying, 'If only...'. It has happened and nothing is going to alter that. You have to avoid becoming bitter, and try to think, 'What's left?' and, 'What can I do to be positive?' Also, and this is important, you must ask yourself, 'What would the person you have lost really want?' Would they want you to sit around moping miserably, feeling your life is ruined? Wouldn't that make them much more unhappy? Wouldn't they be pleased to find that you were going to do your best to carry on as before, and perhaps do that little bit extra in their memory? Perhaps try to do something which you feel they would have wanted.

It's not easy to give advice to people. I can only say what's been helpful to me. We have been through it but one reads every day of all these other terrible things happening. Then one day it happens to you and it makes you realize how terrible it must be for the people who have less support. We have been so lucky in having a closely-knit and large family who have been quite marvellously supportive, and the number of thoughts and messages from all over the world has given a tremendous sense of support, to know that other people are thinking of you. This is why I say to anyone, 'If you hear of somebody who has lost a person near and dear to them, do just write and say you are thinking of them.' It's much easier to bear if you feel that you are not alone, that others are thinking of you. They may be far away, but you are in their thoughts.

Before all this happened, I used to find an excuse for not writing. I would say, 'it's too late', or 'I didn't know them very well', or 'It will be only another letter for them to answer'. Those excuses just don't hold water at all. I now know what a help it is to realize that other people have thought of you and are continuing to think of you even much later. I have not talked about my experiences simply because it happened to my family, but because what we have gone through and our experiences of suffering might be helpful to others in similar circumstances.

Some people might say that I appear strong, but I've been very, very lucky in my parents. I had wonderful parents, and a marvellous grandmother – my father's mother – and then a supremely happy marriage, and seven super children. I now say I have six children here and one in Heaven, where I am sure Nicky is, bless him.

The Very Rev. I.D. Neill CB OBE

Provost Emeritus of Sheffield, the Very Rev. Ivan Neill was born in 1912 and educated at St Dunstan's College, Jesus College, Cambridge (MA) and the London College of Divinity. After serving with the British Expeditionary Force and in the UK during 1941–43, he went overseas again with the 43rd (Wessex) Division, was mentioned in despatches and created Knight Officer of the Order of Orange Nassau (with swords).

After the war he became Senior Chaplain to the Guards Depot at Caterham (1947–50); DACG N. Canal, Egypt (1950–53); followed by further appointments culminating in his appointment as Chaplain General to HM Forces (1960–66). He was also Chaplain to HM the Queen from 1962 to 1966.

Married in 1938, Provost Neill has one son and one daughter.

∞∞∞∞∞∞∞∞∞∞∞∞∞∞∞

I was born and brought up in a Christian home where faith in God was basic to life, and in consequence my experience of God's goodness has been an unfolding one rather than something which began in a dramatic way.

Nevertheless in early youth I was confronted by a love which rectified very serious eye trouble, threatening blindness, and I vividly remember during a sleepless night climbing out of bed in the dark and kneeling down in gratitude and promising heart and life to the Lord Jesus whom I had been taught I must love. I was aged about seven and I told my mother, 'I have given my heart to the Lord Jesus.'

Perhaps I was fortunate in that I did not have to go through that period of agnosticism which is for many the battlefield between a borrowed and a personal faith; but I created my own problems by so often trying to force my God into the limits of my understanding logic and demands. Looking back I ask myself whether it was laziness towards the challenge to incisive thought which protected an otherwise fairly active person, or whether it was the God-given trust in Him which held me. The indebtedness of knowing oneself undeserving and yet accepted, unreliable and yet forgiven and above all loved, somehow makes doubt of one's Lord an unwelcome thought.

Wartime carried its special challenge for me. During childhood and adolescence I had learned to lean on the protection of my God and now I had to face the stark reality that He was not there to protect me personally in danger, but that I was there to serve Him. Throughout the trauma of the Dunkirk withdrawal I carried shamelessly with me that verse from the Psalms which says, 'A thousand shall fall beside thee and ten thousand at thy right hand, but it shall not come nigh thee'. But all the time I was secretly ashamed – a shame which has never left me.

Fear was in my heart and I knew it. I feared for myself far more than for those to whom I belonged as chaplain. The brief encounters at Louvain had been dangerous, but the comradeship in danger had well-nigh removed all fear. Now we were ordered to withdraw. Our Belgian liaison officer burnt the Union Jack openly outside Louvain Town Hall as we retired. What did it mean? Our first stop was outside Brussels and many soldiers marched there in their sleep. I had a light Austin car and a driver and I didn't feel proud of myself. At Roubaix I picked up a fine officer whose courage had snapped and I wondered if I too was not listening to the voice of fear. Our lines of communication had been destroyed. No ammunition was getting through – neither was food, although we fed on the land as we passed through the deserted country.

There were times when something positive could be done such as raiding the food depot of NAAFI where everyone had fled and so getting some three tons of food to the lines, but I knew I was growing apart from the fighting man and being just part of our own Headquarters. Knowing we were heading for the coast, survival rather than service was too much in mind. I had cause to be dissatisfied. I felt I had not been mature enough for the trust. If the regiment did not notice this it was because of their generosity. I was never confronted with it then or later. But I felt ashamed.

It was later, preparing ourselves as chaplains for the counter-invasion of Normandy that I had to face the knowledge of my shameless self-preservation and overcome my personal fear. Some twelve of us chaplains spent a day together in Tenterden in Kent where our Division was working up for our invasion of Normandy. We knew we were ministering to some 17,000 men, many of whom would die. We finally knelt together offering our lives to the Lord who had given His Life to us, we surrendered to Him our self-protection and fears, and we knew that if we survived our lives were still 'not ours'. Before crossing the Rhine we reaffirmed this together by which time three of us had died and five were wounded and out of the line, but none had flinched in the face of danger.

Still I remember the agony of heart and mind when leading a gathering of officers and men in worship in the words, 'the whole Earth is full of thy Glory,' when all were in slit trenches bordering a small field and high explosives were interrupting the peace we prayed about. This, in one guise or another, was to be a frequent experience.

I was one of those who survived the war and returned home to resume civilian life. To that extent it may be said that I won through, but now in retirement I am conscious more of the gaps in my ministry than of any achievements; I have been extraordinarily privileged through the course of life in countless ways, and have known the friendly support of those under whose authority I served. But this was even more so when related to a Father in Heaven who knew full well one's weaknesses and deficiencies but who still offered only pardon, love, guiding and enabling power. And now, well on in years I would want to write in simple and grateful faith, 'I know whom I have believed and am persuaded that He is able to keep that which I have committed to Him against that day.'

Juliet Pannett FRSA

Juliet Pannett is a renowned British portrait painter whose commissions include the Princes Andrew and Edward for HM the Queen. For many official bodies she has painted countless public figures, including Princess Marina, Princess Alexandra, Sir Douglas Bader, Sir Adrian Boult, Lord Butler, Lord Goodman, Patrick Moore, Lord Tonypandy and, to date, no less than nine Prime Ministers.

Juliet Pannett has held exhibitions in London, Coventry, Gloucester, Bath, Brighton, New York, Cleveland (Ohio), and Hong Kong and has exhibited at the Royal Academy, the Royal Society of Portrait Painters, the Royal Institute of Painters in Watercolour and others. She was also the official artist on Qantas Inaugural Jet Flights London to Sydney (1959), London to Hong Kong (1964) and Air Canada Inaugural Flights London to Vancouver (1968). Her paintings are on permanent exhibition in the National Portrait Gallery, Oxford and Cambridge colleges and many other galleries throughout the United Kingdom.

In the following narrative Juliet Pannett relates her struggle to resume her career after some years without painting, while bringing up her family.

I was fortunate that I was able to do what I really wanted from my earliest years, for I always had the encouragement of my parents. I am told that I began to draw when I was very young and I remember clearly an idea I carried out at the age of six. I carefully removed the bottom of a matchbox, replacing it with some fairly thin paper exactly cut to size. On this I drew and painted two little children crossing a river on a rather shaky wooden bridge. On the back of this piece of paper, towards the top of it, I had drawn and painted an angel, complete with long white robe and halo. To get the full effect you had to open the matchbox and hold it up to the light, whereupon you immediately became aware of the Guardian Angel, and this is what it was called. I developed this theme in several different ways, and it is still a family joke.

When I was twelve I joined the Sussex County Cricket Club, and it wasn't long before I was drawing the players for the Sussex County Magazine. I was paid one guinea for each one published, and I felt rich and successful; I continued to draw local characters, among them a large family of gypsies who camped on the downs behind Worthing.

On leaving school at sixteen I went straight to the Brighton School of Art, where I studied life painting under Louis Ginnett, an excellent artist and teacher, one to whom I certainly owe much. I married in 1938; my husband was a regular Army Officer who had been through the First World War and after serving seven years in India he retired. He was recalled for the Second World War but was in England all the time, so my children and I were able to follow him to his various stations.

After the war we found that we had very little money. My husband retired again almost at once, and his army pension was not generous. I was unable to add to the family coffers, for during the years Denis and Liz were young I had no time for painting. I did, however, find a few ways of adding small, but none-the-less welcome amounts; I remember, for instance, picking up bits of metal from the streets. There was quite a lot lying about in those days, and I hate waste anyway! So I picked up every little piece I saw and popped each one into the pram to bring home. When I had collected enough I sold it for a very modest sum at the nearest scrap metal depot. Clean waste paper was valuable in those days, so I also collected newspapers to sell. My husband had taken on a job at quite a low salary, teaching in a boys' prep. school, and every penny had to be considered.

Happy though I was looking after my family, the urge to paint again was still strong and growing. The frustration was too much for me and I had a kind of a breakdown. My voice went completely and I became depressed. The local hospital could find nothing wrong but my marvellous doctor advised me to start painting again, whatever the difficulties – and he was right.

But how was I to get back into the art world after several years devoted to raising a family which left no time for painting or even for maintaining my contacts in the art world? We had no car and I had no studio, but we did have a garage, so we painted the walls white, put in a window and there was my working studio. I started going to London from Croydon, where we lived, to paint war-damaged buildings, and when I had done enough I carried large, heavy portfolios up to London to submit my work to various houses, and I took framed pictures up to exhibitions.

I sent an old portrait of my husband to the Royal Society of Portrait Painters and they hung it. Sir Malcolm Sargent happened to be at the exhibition, and I screwed up my courage and asked his permission to sketch at one of his rehearsals. This led to my sketching a number of orchestras at rehearsal and I eventually submitted three paintings of well-known conductors and their orchestras to the Britain in Watercolour Exhibition. This was another step forward as they were seen there by the Art Editor of the *Illustrated London News* who, as a result, appointed me as a Special Artist to the magazine in succession to Bryan de Grineau, who had recently died.

I was given their ticket for the Press Gallery at the House of Commons, where I had my own seat from which I was allowed to sketch Members of Parliament. This was the first time that anyone had ever been allowed to draw in the House. This soon led to further assignments, which included two Inaugural Flights to Australia with Qantas and two further Inaugural Flights with Air Canada, all as Official Artist.

In due course royal portraits followed, first Princess Marina in 1968, and in 1974 Princes Andrew and Edward, and Princess Alexandra in 1983. Quite recently I have been commissioned to paint an oil portrait of Her Majesty the Queen, which I hope to carry out as soon as Her Majesty's official engagements allow.

In my work I have met many outstanding people; surgeons, dancers, musicians, Prime Ministers, Service heads, Heads of Schools and businessmen have been among my sitters. Mine have been years of great interest and, I am glad to say, of much work, every moment of which I have enjoyed.

I shall always be grateful to that doctor who pushed me into overcoming seemingly insurmountable obstacles to fight my way back into the art world. It is also a happy thought that this change of priority, rather than harm my children, gave them an example to follow, for they have both grown up to become established and successful professional artists in their own right.

David Shepherd OBE FRSA

Born in 1931 and educated at Stowe, David Shepherd started his career as an aviation artist and was a founder member of the Association of Aviation Artists. In 1960 he began painting African wildlife and held his first one-man show in London in 1962, a second in 1965 and exhibited in Johannesburg in 1966 and 1969. He has also painted portraits of HM the Queen Mother (for The King's Regiment), Dr Kenneth Kaunda, President of Zambia and HE Sheikh Zaid of Abu Dhabi.

In the USA in 1971 he raised sufficient funds from the auction of his paintings to purchase a helicopter to combat game-poaching in Zambia and two years later raised a further £127,500 for Operation Tiger with his painting 'Tiger Fire'. In 1979 he was made a Member of Honour of the World Wildlife Fund, and was awarded the Order of The Golden Ark by HRH Prince Bernhard in 1973.

In addition to his unique services to wildlife conservation, David Shepherd has enjoyed a lifelong love affair with steam locomotives and, after being presented with an 1896 locomotive by President Kaunda, he purchased two further steam locomotives from British Rail in 1967 and formed the East Somerset Railway. This was the beginning of the saga of crises which he relates so vividly in the following pages.

∞∞∞∞∞∞∞∞∞∞∞∞∞

I am so unmechanical, I cannot even mend a fuse when the power goes off. I am an impulsive sort of chap, and I suppose it was inevitable, therefore, that when I picked up the telephone in 1967 and asked British Railways if I could buy two of their enormous 135-ton steam locomotives, my life would change, for the better, and for the worse. After all, you can't do that sort of thing without it having some effect on your personal life!

This is not the place to go into the whole saga of what followed, except to say that a love-hate relationship immediately began to develop quickly between myself and *Black Prince*, the bigger of the two locomotives – the big one weighs 140 tons and the baby one weights 137 tons! This great monster, in full working order when I purchased her, has, since those days, meant almost as much to me as my wife and four daughters. It is amazing how fond one can get of a steam locomotive when you see the pleasure it gives to countless thousands of people. However, she, and the Inland Revenue combined, were responsible for the moment in 1970 when my finances and my mental worries took a dive to their lowest point. (Success in my life as a professional painter has not only brought its great fulfilment and joy, but it has also brought its attendant problems.)

From that telephone call, ultimately, the East Somerset Railway at Cranmore in Somerset was born. A registered charity, it runs steam-hauled passenger trains to a schedule over several miles of track and, I am happy to say, gives enormous pleasure to a lot of people. However, a steam railway is the biggest financial 'sponge' in the world. The rate at which such an enterprise soaks up money is matched by the pace at which *Black Prince* eats up coal, 'black gold'. In spite of the dedicated efforts of our marvellous team of volunteers on the railway, the day came when *Black Prince* finally had to have an overhaul. With our limited facilities, and the workshop full with another engine being overhauled anyway, she had to go away for the job to be done. In spite of help from many quarters, the cost of this exercise sky-rocketed beyond my deepest fears and seemed to escalate by the minute.

I don't smoke, I don't gamble and, at the most, I have one or two drinks every week. I don't think that is excessive. However, I suppose some people could think that I was extravagant. I don't think so, because I paid £3,000 for *Black Prince* and she is now worth £80,000! Nevertheless, before I learned the hard way, I did have the habit of spending money before I earned it and, in the early 1970s moreover, my finances had not been handled as well as they might have been, bearing in mind my extrovert nature. (I was the bank's best customer!) The crisis happened in 1976. At the same time as the engineering company overhauling *Black Prince* kept asking for more and more and more money as the job was bigger than they thought, the Inland Revenue caught me up. The insatiable demands by them had overtaken me, and I had not been making any provision for the future. This particular demand was enough to keep several families well fed for many years and they wanted it now. At that same moment, my new friend and family solicitor, my financial advisor, took over my affairs and told me very bluntly that I had to behave myself from that minute on and that I was not to write a cheque for more than a few hundred pounds without telling him, otherwise the bank would foreclose. I would have to sell *Black Prince*, knock over our magnificent Victorian steam locomotive shed and sell the brick rubble and tear up the track and sell it to a scrap merchant. I told him that I had posted an enormous cheque to the Inland Revenue. 'Now you've gone and done it – you're sunk!' 'Well, what could I do – they will charge me interest if I don't send the money off to them?' 'Well, I'll have to go back to the bank tomorrow, spend all day being nice to them, but I don't hold out much hope.'

I am an emotional sort of chap, I burst into tears, walked down to the bottom of the garden and cried my heart out. I went back to the studio, and, the next day painted one of the best paintings of elephants that I have ever done!

I always paint better in a crisis. I learned a lot that evening. The Inland Revenue got their money. My solicitor taught me a lesson which I will never ever forget and the bank did not foreclose. I dragged myself up from those hairy moments and, working every hour that God gave me, paid off the bank. I am no longer their best customer! *Black Prince* was overhauled and is now back in full glory on the East Somerset Railway.

Dinah Sheridan

Born in London of a Russian father and German mother, Dinah Sheridan had her stage training at the Italia Conti School and first gained public acclaim in her early films *Where No Vultures Fly* and the immortal *Genevieve*. By her marriage to the late Jimmy Hanley, she has two children, Jeremy Hanley, MP and senior lecturer in accountancy and Jenny Hanley, TV actress and presenter. After an absence of some years, she returned to films in 1970, with the leading part in *The Railway Children*, since when she has featured continuously in television and on the London stage. She is now married to Canadian-born actor, Jack Merivale.

∞∞∞∞∞∞∞∞∞∞∞∞

'Does this mean we have to live in Switzerland?' My mother was looking very worried indeed, but the doctor did not encourage her at all. 'She won't reach Switzerland, I think you should try Broadstairs.'

My parents were deeply upset. To a refugee Russian and a German, living in Hampstead with two small girls and trying to exist on a meagre salary gained from selling kitchen gadgets door to door, the idea of moving once again must have been daunting. But I had contracted TB tummy glands and Broadstairs was the only answer. The air was cold; the wind blew hard and strong straight from the North Sea; as near to the atmosphere of a Swiss mountain without the added journey.

We settled into a ground floor flat on the seafront. It had the requirements for my mother or father to carry me from my bed to my spinal carriage in which I was to live during daylight hours. This new 'home' had a hood. Large and black, it encased me in its rubbery smell when the rain lashed down. Covered to the nose in many blankets, I had my own world in there; lonely except for my much-loved woolly bear, Mischa. The wicker-work smelled too, an individual woody smell, which is still brought back to me today as I go shopping with my basket on wheels. The days when the sun shone and I lay with few coverings were a happy contrast. With a handmirror I could watch what was going on – a twist of my wrist and I could see my sister and her friends playing games, swimming, jumping, all the things I was going to do. I never doubted that.

The day came when I was taught to walk again. My muscles were painfully weak but with my family's help I made daily resolutions to get further across the room, to negotiate corners, even to tackle a few stairs. Now for school. I had envied my sister so much as she set off to the local kindergarten and could not wait to join her. Unfortunately I entered into everything with far too much vigour and was forced to return to my confinement. Not for long this time – but having tested the excitement of grown-up reading, my blankets now were stuffed with books – and Shakespeare. A spinal library carriage!

Why I wanted to go on the stage, how I knew what a stage career might be like, I cannot say. Shakespeare had been devoured, but not understood surely. Nevertheless this was my decision; I was going to be an actress. My poor parents who had sacrificed so much for me were appalled. No, it was far too strenuous; did I want to be ill again?

I was now a determined ten-year-old. My parents, in an effort to frustrate my theatrical ambitions, took me to a sleazy pantomime in the nearby town of Margate, in the hope that this would subdue some desires. It was a very poor production, and as we emerged into the night air, mama turned to me triumphantly, 'There! You wouldn't want to be in a production like that would you?' 'No,' I replied, 'but that's not what I mean by the theatre.' I was born a Virgo and Virgos are obstinate.

The following Christmas time my German grandmother, who by now also lived in England, invited us all to the Holborn Empire in London to see *Where The Rainbow Ends*. The train journey, the lights of the big city, the sumptuous auditorium, it was all magic. The overture set the mood for me and as the curtains rose I was lost in another world. This was the theatre I meant. This was the theatre world I was going to join. The play was put on every Christmas by the owner of a children's stage school, Italia Conti and it was she who was to start me on the road to my dreams. Within a year I was also on that stage, dancing as a dragonfly and a moth and understudying the girl on the steps. At that time I felt I had achieved the highest peak of the profession! Once a week I would travel by myself from Broadstairs for lessons in elocution and dancing of all kinds – I was strong, healthy, and launched.

Obstinacy? Courage? Perhaps a little of the one and not knowingly any of the other. I like to think that it is determination and unswerving knowledge of where one's dedication lies. To know what you want to do and to overcome all obstacles.

Rosemary Anne Sisson

Playwright, author, scriptwriter, Rosemary Anne Sisson is the daughter of the late Professor C.J. Sisson. Educated at Cheltenham Ladies College, University College, London (BA Hons English) and Newnham College, Cambridge (MLitt), she served in the Second World War before taking up appointments as Lecturer in English. Her first play, *The Queen and the Welshman*, was produced at the Lyric Hammersmith in 1957. Several plays later she began writing for TV and contributed to such series as *The Six Wives of Henry VIII, Upstairs Downstairs, A Town Like Alice* and *The Irish RM*. She is currently engaged in creating a new television series, *The Bretts*. She wrote many film scripts for Walt Disney and has published a number of children's books. In 1979–80 she was co-chairman of the Writers Guild of Great Britain.

Her great success as a writer was destined almost from babyhood. At the age of six she was sending poems to her father's friends, Walter de la Mare and A.A. Milne.

The only thing I ever wanted to do was to be an actress. But the war came when I was fifteen and everything I had planned came to a halt – so far as I was concerned, my life was ended. So, instead of pursuing my dream, I took a secretarial course after leaving school and began working in the RAF as a civilian. Proudly, I rose to the status of what I called administrative secretary, which was officially Clerk (G.D.), but I felt I could not let the war go by without doing something more active, so I joined the WAAF and they put me in the Royal Observer Corps.

After the war ended I, like everyone else I knew, felt terribly old and terribly beaten. I was hungry, my memory seemed to have deserted me, I had no courage and I felt just 'done for'. My father had been to America and one of his friends, a professor at the University of Wisconsin, invited me to go over and take a post there as a junior lecturer. I was then at Cambridge, taking a postgraduate degree in English – the only subject I knew – and I cabled back saying, 'If you can wait a year, I can come with an MLitt.' I never did get my PhD, but I went with my MLitt and really that is when life began again for me.

In fact, it started on the way over. After all those years of food rationing and shortage of nourishment, on the boat there was more food than one could eat, which in a way was horrifying. But the thing I found most wonderful in America in 1949 was that anything was possible there. We had got into such a state in England of saying, 'You can't do that, don't you know there's a war on?' But in America it was not just the fact of there being plenty of everything, but that they took it for granted and that whatever you set your mind to do, was possible.

I stayed for a year – and I worked on a ranch in the summer, which again was enjoyable, frightening and fascinating – and I came home feeling quite a different creature. However, I was still a university lecturer, which was not my ambition. I loved the work, but I still felt lost and unfulfilled. It was second best.

My parents then moved to Stratford-upon-Avon, where my father, a Professor of English and a Shakespeare Scholar, had been invited to be Senior Fellow of the Shakespeare Institute. For him it was a wonderful second career at the very end of his life. He had always done a lot of administration and the students had always been rather afraid of him. But here at

Stratford he had postgraduate students and for the first time in his whole career they teased him. They loved him and, as never before, he treated them in the same way and he became to them just as he was to us, a funny, loving man, and he had the happiest ten years of his life. It was a wonderful and joyous period for the whole family. I managed, no doubt with some parental influence, to transfer from University College, London, to the University of Birmingham for a year, and for the first time I found myself in the thick of the Theatre. I met young actors and I remember, after going to one particularly enjoyable gathering, coming home and writing in my diary, 'These are my people, this is my life.'

But even then, I was not in it myself – I was only an onlooker. Until the day when, after seeing Richard Burton in *Henry V*, I went away and looked up the historical references, which disclosed the events leading up to the Tudor Dynasty – the story which Shakespeare did not write. So I wrote it, in Shakespearean blank verse, with about forty-eight characters, confident that it would make a most suitable vehicle for John Gielgud. Of course, it came back several times from managements and I constantly rewrote it, until Glen Byam Shaw kindly read it, invited me out to lunch, and gave me an invaluable lesson in basic playwriting. Three years and seven rewrites later, *The Queen and the Welshman* was produced on the Fringe of the Edinburgh Festival.

Now I knew my job was not to act in plays myself, but to write plays for others to act in. From that moment I was happy and, however badly things went for me after that, I knew I was doing what I wanted to do. Success certainly didn't come easily or quickly. The thud of the returned script on the mat and the cold, printed rejection-slip was a fearful test of courage and self-confidence. At one point I wrote in my diary, 'I don't know how long I can go on getting knocked down and still get up again.' But *The Queen and the Welshman* led to *The Six Wives of Henry VIII* and that led to *Upstairs, Downstairs*, and there came, at last, a time when, having said my usual prayer, 'O Lord, let me be a success,' I suddenly said to myself, 'I really think I am!'

But then there is the other side of the coin. Either I am grumbling because I cannot get my plays on the stage or, paradoxically, I am getting too many commissions to write television series based on other people's ideas, and have no leisure to write plays of my own. When you are a writer you always have your failures. You can never afford to get complacent and that is what is good for you. I am never satisfied and never should be, but I do know now that I have done what I wanted to do with my life, and that is the greatest gift that God can give.

Wayne Sleep

Born in Plymouth in 1948 and educated in Hartlepool, Wayne Sleep entered the Royal Ballet School as a Leverhulme Scholar at the age of twelve, and graduated into the Royal Ballet in 1966. He became a soloist in 1970 and a Principal in 1973. In 1978 he left the Royal Ballet to form his own group of dancers and has since popularized his individual style of production and choreography in shows such as *DASH*, *Cats*, *Song and Dance* and *Cabaret*.

Wayne Sleep has also appeared in a number of films, has choreographed and performed in many television shows and the *Hot Shoe Show* series. In 1983 he was voted Show Business Personality of the Year.

∽∽∽∽∽∽∽∽∽∽∽∽∽∽∽∽∽∽

I was very lucky getting into the Royal Ballet School. Coming from a working class family, we had no money and could not afford to pay, but I won a scholarship and joined the School at the age of twelve.

All went well until I was sixteen, when I was to be considered for the Royal Ballet Company. Unfortunately I had not grown very tall and it was touch and go as to whether I would be accepted. However, once again I was lucky. I had worked very hard during my time at the school and I think because of that Ninette de Valois and Frederick Ashton thought I had potential and let me in, although I was really far too short. That was in 1966.

There were, of course, certain roles I could not dance, owing to my lack of height. Roles specially created for a dancer are few and far between. So after twelve years in the company, as I did not continue to grow, I decided to branch out and form my own group. This was partly due to not having enough roles to dance, but also because I could see there were other dancers – brilliant jazz dancers and others, who never got a chance to dance, except in commercials or in variety shows, where they might be one of ten, like moving wallpaper – background to a single star.

Another factor was that the dance medium had not been given a proper airing on television and I found it a very severe handicap that as a trained dancer you only fitted into certain traditional situations, such as a ballet company or perhaps the odd film, in which you were unlikely to be featured.

The situation with dance in England is very strange. In this country we have excellent training. We have good schools and a wonderful ballet company, but although the English love dancing – look how they are always talking about Fred Astaire and Gene Kelly – they do nothing to promote and encourage their own people. I found this extremely odd. You could train all your life for dancing and then find that the television companies aren't interested and nobody seems keen to put on a dance show.

So I decided to take the plunge and back my own belief that the British public would patronize dance if they liked what was offered. I formed my group. We produced a show and on our first tour we packed every house all over Britain!

As a result of this success, the *Hot Shoe Show* was produced by the BBC. They had assumed there was no audience for this kind of entertainment and we, the dancers, had proved them wrong. I knew all along that there must be a demand, because everybody always professed to love the dance, and now it had been proved.

Nevertheless, I still find it a constant struggle to keep dance before the British public. The Arts Council and sponsoring organizations are very peculiar in the way they spend their money. They finance young, inexperienced groups to undertake major tours around the country, which is the surest way to deter audiences – especially first time audiences – from coming again, when they think what they have seen is the best the medium can offer. A better policy would be to allow these young groups to experiment and improve their work and only then to use the balance of the subsidy to do one tour per year.

To maintain and expand the popularity of dance in this country, such experimentation is absolutely essential. This I earnestly believe, and to back my belief I have ploughed back such money as I have had by buying a studio just for this purpose. There we shall continue to do experimental work, to explore new techniques and constantly improve what we put before the public.

The difficulties for dancers are unending, but I think if you love something enough you are prepared to put up with them. Prospects are brighter than they were. Before the advent of *DASH, Cats, Song and Dance* and the television *Hot Shoe Show*, no dancer would dare to leave a ballet company, because there wasn't much work for them elsewhere. Now at least, there are opportunities for those who feel they are not making headway in traditional ballet or not being used to the best advantage.

The thing is to make whatever you have work for you. Even if it appears at first to be a handicap, try and turn it to your advantage and never give up. In my own case, it was lack of height which forced me to strike out on my own, using such talent as I have in new ways, which I might never have had the opportunity or incentive to discover in normal circumstances.

The Rev. The Lord Soper
MA PhD

Donald Soper was educated at Aske's School, Hatcham, before going up to St Catherine's College, Cambridge, where he graduated as MA and studied for the Ministry at Wesley House, Cambridge. He then read for his PhD at the London School of Economics.

Three years as Minister at the South London Mission were followed by a further seven years at the Central London Mission. In 1936 he was appointed Superintendent of the Central London Mission at Kingsway Hall, where he served until 1978. During this period he was President of the Methodist Conference in 1953 and Chairman of Shelter from 1974–78. Created a Life Peer in 1965, he is President of the League Against Cruel Sports and in 1981 he received the Peace Award of the World Methodist Council.

Lord Soper is the author of a number of books on various aspects of the Christian faith. He is married and has four daughters. In the following article he recalls the time when, as an undergraduate, he became 'a reluctant but inevitable atheist' and how he won the battle to regain his faith.

∞∞∞∞∞∞∞∞∞∞∞∞∞∞∞∞

The book was called *The History of Rationalism* and it was the reading of it that was both the occasion and the cause of one of the most acute crises of my life; and certainly the one which provoked the most radical change in my mental state. As a boy I grew up in a Christian home where religion was predominant, and its various practices, such as sabbatarianism, were the inclusive methods by which it was expressed. Moreover, as my adolescence coincided with the period of the First World War, my life was inevitably restricted. I lived as everybody did in an occupied country – not occupied as France was by the enemy, but shut in by the exigencies and demands of the siege mentality that is always the accompaniment of national armed conflict. One of the effects of this claustrophobia was that my own attitude to the Christian faith and indeed my subscription to it, though constantly challenged from inside, was not questioned from outside. Because it was not so challenged I tended to accept its main propositions as not only unchallenged, but unchallengeable. My Christian faith remained in this cocooned condition while I was still at school and living at home. Then I was fortunate enough to win an exhibition to Cambridge University and I left home for the first time.

It was within this new unprecedented environment that for the first time I felt a stranger in a strange land. In no respect was this estrangement so catastrophic as in the realm of my beliefs. A college friend, a friend in disguise and a very thorough disguise it turned out to be, lent me *The History of Rationalism* to read. I ploughed through it with an ever increasing dismay. One by one my assured convictions were demolished, and by the time I came to its last page I was a reluctant but inevitable atheist. I know now that this so-called 'history of rationalism' is a very questionable document, and today, were I to read it for the first time, I would be satisfied that the reasons for faith are considerably more cogent than their repudiations by the agnostics or the atheists. At the age of eighteen, however, I was unprepared for the assault and the battle was lost, and unfortunately I was unaware of the truism, 'one battle may be lost but there is time to win another.' I now realize how true that claim is, and better still how I came to recover a faith more satisfying than the one which I had lost.

The first element in that recovery was almost purely circumstantial. From my earliest years the church was my second home. I was as much at home at church, Sunday school, prayer meeting, Bible class and choir practice as in our dining room and my bedroom.

Therefore, when I reached Cambridge it was as natural for me to find a church as a college. This I did. I presented myself to the local Methodist Minister, informed the Sunday School Superintendent that I would be available to take a 'class' on Sunday afternoons, and made arrangements to join in the church activities alongside my college regime. Then the blow fell. I no longer believed, which of course completely altered my relationship with organized Christianity in most respects but by no means all of them. Church was still home to me and I had no desire to leave home merely because I had become allergic to the food. I felt it only right to acquaint the Sunday School Superintendent with the revolutionary change that had happened to me. I told him that I could not, in honour, become a Sunday School teacher. He saw the point at once and seemed to think 'that was that', but not for me. I had no intention of leaving the church just because I had become an atheist. I suggested that though I could not teach a class I might play the piano for the hymns. That superintendent was an understanding man. He agreed and all the time I remained an unbeliever in Christianity, I regularly played its hymns – though this somewhat bizarre association did not last for very long.

Gradually I came to appreciate the adventure of believing rather than the false security of an unthinking acquiescence in dogma. Even more significantly I came to realize how much more there is in the Christian life than that part of it which can be rationally expressed. Above all, as the new world of university life developed I learned that 'he that doeth the will shall know of the Gospel.' It would be untrue to say that the body of Christian doctrine remained, for me, intact. I found that there is a place for agnosticism as well as conviction in a measured faith. It would not be presumptuous of me, I hope, to claim that the crisis through which I passed served to prove to me the truth in the word of Jesus; that we are first to seek the Kingdom of God, for only by so doing can we find, in discovering that Kingdom, everything else is also to be found. For me the church in Cambridge was God's Kingdom for me. I had made that discovery, without fully appreciating it, from my earliest years. It stood me in good and sufficient stead in my crisis of faith, more than fifty years ago, and it has been my ever deepening conviction as the years have passed.

Wing Cmdr. R. Stanford-Tuck DSO DFC (2 bars)

Wing Commander Robert Stanford-Tuck, born in 1916, was educated at St Dunstan's Prep. School and College, Reading. After leaving school he spent two years at sea as a cadet before joining the RAF in 1935. He served with No.65 Fighter Squadron until the outbreak of war, was posted to 92 (F) Squadron and shot down eight enemy aircraft during the Dunkirk evacuation. Promoted to Wing Commander with No.257 Burma Fighter Squadron he commanded Wings at Duxford and Biggin Hill until he was captured in 1942. Awarded the DSO and the DFC with two bars, his official record lists twenty-seven confirmed victories, eight probably destroyed, six damaged; wounded once, baled out four times.

Wing Commander Stanford-Tuck tells the story of his capture and his unceasing efforts, over more than three years, to escape.

∞∞∞∞∞∞∞∞∞∞∞∞∞∞

The twenty-eighth of January 1942 was a dark, cloudy day, a day ideal for what we called a 'Rhubarb' operation, in which we shot across the Channel, dived out of the cloud to shoot up pre-arranged targets and then climbed back into the dark before the Messerschmitts arrived.

I was doing a low-level attack, with cannon and machine guns, in a Spitfire and had just blown up my target, an alcohol distillery. As I came out towards Boulogne I saw a big, fat train shunting up and down by the marshalling yards. I still had some ammunition, which I thought I might as well use up; I blew the train in all directions and I was just turning up the valley, at nought feet, right on the deck, when every gun, cannon and light flak opened up all along the valley at me.

It hit the Spitfire through the sump and the engine and it was an awful mess. I was doing about 300 m.p.h. when they hit me but to try to pull out would have been useless. I would lose speed and be a sitting duck for all the guns again. Suddenly, straight ahead there appeared one of those lovely flat French fields. I didn't hesitate. I smacked the plane down on its belly and it skidded to a halt, without turning over.

I was right in the middle of a German gun battery and men were running towards me from all sides. I leant into the cockpit to try and destroy my maps but my lighter refused to work. At that moment one of the Germans put a bullet through the fuselage, just missing my bottom and I judged it was time to put up my hands and be captured.

They were a bit rough at first, because I had hit one of their guns very badly and killed all the crew, I'm afraid. The soldiers grabbed me, pushing and shoving me about – a very rough lot they looked, too – and I thought they were going to beat me up. Fortunately a young officer appeared and cooled them all down. I was marched off to the local village, searched and popped into a little cell for the night.

It was to be more than three years before I got back home to England again and during that long period of captivity my one constant obsession was escape – an obsession shared with all my other fellow prisoners, wherever we were. I decided from the start that my only positive course was to harass the enemy in every way open to me, and opportunities constantly occurred. At Dulag Luft, my first prison camp, I swore at those interrogating me, I smashed up my cell and on one occasion actually succeeded, by yelling and banging my shoe on the cell wall, in stopping the man next door from giving information. This was an American who, after weeks of incessant questioning, was about to crack and my shouting at him through the wall just pulled the poor devil together in time.

This little performance resulted in my being recorded as a bad influence and moved to Spangenberg. This was a medieval castle, a Walt Disney affair, with walls about two feet thick and battlements. It had an enormous dry moat, very wide and very deep all round it and to prevent any efforts to escape they had a lot of wild boars grazing down there. We used to feed them razor blades stuck into rotten potatoes, but they didn't seem to mind – it never made any of them even cough!

When I joined I found they were all senior staff officers there, led by General Fortune of the 51st Highland Division and although there was absolutely no chance of escape I continued to make myself a frightful nuisance to our captors. We made booby traps for the sentries, we adopted a policy of 'go slow' and got up to every trick we could think of and after a few weeks a number of us were removed, this time to Stalag Luft III, the main Air Force camp housing over 2,000 prisoners. Here there were innumerable escape projects going on all the time. Uniforms were remade into workmen's suits, papers were forged and there was an internal organization which vetted each scheme in advance, to judge the feasibility and to avoid clashing.

The attempt I personally remember best was when I planned, together with a Polish flight lieutenant, to escape in the refuse cart. We had an old German peasant, with an equally clapped out old horse and cart, who used to collect the refuse from the waste bins. With the help of the escape committee we arranged for the old boy to be entertained with tea and a cigarette for a few minutes each morning while we took the measurements of the cart and designed and made a sort of shield, or false bottom, out of any suitable material at hand. This was intended to fit part way down the sloping sides of the cart and protect and hide us as we lay hidden under it.

On the appointed day we leapt into the cart and made ourselves comfortable, lying down under our shield, while our chaps entertained the dopey driver, who was by now accustomed to his ten-minute break over a cup of tea and a cigarette in one of the nearby huts. Eventually the old boy came out and started shovelling rubbish into the cart and we were looking forward to being driven out of camp in a short time. But a snag developed. The home-made platform above us was not strong enough to bear the increasing weight that kept coming in and before long we were squashed absolutely flat. It was very unpleasant – just like being buried alive – and it stank to high heaven. At last we could stand it no longer. We gave a yell and fortunately the old peasant cottoned on. He led his horse round to the back of a hut and our chaps hauled us out.

It was at Stalug Luft III that the Germans unwittingly saved my life. We had been working for over a year on a major escape plan called Tom, Dick and Harry, a plan involving a number of tunnels, some of which were discovered from time to time and others abandoned after falls of earth. The Germans suspected that I was among those who were up to no good and about three weeks before the break was timed to take place they read out twenty names at roll call one morning, mine included, marched us into a truck and drove us up to another camp called Belaria. I later learned that the escape plan had been discovered and the Germans had shot twenty of those caught in the tunnel, including Roger Bushell, the head of the escape organization and the young Belgian captain who went with him in my place.

Exactly three years from the day of my capture – 28 January 1945 – the Germans, pressed by the Russian advance from the east, marched us all off due west and in the chaotic conditions that followed – heavy snow, shortage of food, disease and low German morale – I managed to cut loose, together with a Polish friend, and make contact with the Russians. Here again, luck was on my side, because I speak Russian and was able to explain our position. Poland, Moscow, back to Poland again and finally by ship from Odessa, to be reunited with my fiancée at last.

Wartime flying is a rough old game. On one side you have the high excitement of battle and the constant exhilaration of pitting your skill against the enemy. On the other side the tragic loss of close friends and the sadness when they don't return at the end of the day. I am not a religious man. I believe it is the duty of every man to feel responsible for himself and not to look for outside help. But I must say it is quite surprising, this thing which we call luck. The little lady sits on your shoulder – Lady Luck – and it doesn't matter how darn good you are, how well-trained, skilful or daring, if she is not there when you need her, you are lost.

Dr Miriam Stoppard MD MRCP

Dr Miriam Stoppard, the well-known writer and broadcaster on health care, was a State Scholar of Newcastle-upon-Tyne Central High School, before studying medicine at the Royal Free Hospital School of Medicine, where she was awarded the prize for Experimental Physiology in 1958, qualifying MB at Durham University in 1961. After two years at Kings College Hospital, Newcastle, and successive appointments in Chemical Pathology and Dermatology, Dr Stoppard joined a pharmaceutical company in 1968 and was Managing Director from 1977–81. She has written a number of books on health care for babies, children and adults, has published over forty papers in medical journals and has made a significant contribution to the understanding of health problems through her television and radio programmes.

Dr Stoppard is married to the playwright, Tom Stoppard, and has two sons and two stepsons.

∞∞∞∞∞∞∞∞∞∞∞∞∞∞

As a newly qualified doctor, I set my sights on getting the MRCP degree. This stands for Member of the Royal College of Physicians. It's a postgraduate degree, so that you have to study while working full time for three or four years before you are ready to take it. It's the Holy Grail of medicine, it's the seal of merit. Without it you cannot climb up the promotional ladder, and for a woman there's simply no question that you will achieve senior status without it.

After eighteen months, the consultant for whom I was working suggested that I had a try. I was quite unprepared and I failed. Next morning, on the long hospital corridor, the consultant sympathetically put his hand on my shoulder and said, 'Don't worry Miriam, if you'd passed it first time none of us would speak to you.'

So I settled down to the really hard work and burned much midnight oil. A year later I decided to try again and this time I felt I was prepared.

The MRCP system is in various parts, each part having to be taken in London. As I worked in Bristol this meant journeying to and fro after being hailed by telegram saying that I had passed the previous part. If you were not in this fortunate group the MRCP sent out a peremptory telegram which ran something like this: 'The standard you have reached so far in the MRCP examination is such that there is no point in your proceeding with it further.'

My telegram was to arrive at the Bristol University Students' Union, and I well remember the morning. I'd collected the telegram, I walked out of the Union and stood on the wide stone steps with my husband behind me and opened the telegram. It said more or less what is written above.

I burst into tears and stormed off. To blazes with the exam. I cursed the MRCP, I cursed the examination, I cursed the examiners. Who needed it? I could get on without it. Who wanted to be part of such an unfair system? (The pass rate is five per cent.)

My husband stood by patiently while I ranted and raved and when I'd finished he said, 'I hope you realize that the exam is specially designed for people like you. They don't want failures, they want people who get up and try again.'

It took me a week to realize that he was right. It took me much less time to realize that I really needed the MRCP qualification. So I got up and I tried again and a year later I got it.

Lance Thirkell

Born in Australia in 1921, the son of Angela Thirkell the novelist, he was educated at St Paul's School and Magdalen College Oxford. With the Essex Yeomanry he fought in the Second World War from D-day to the Rhine and then in SE Asia with the Royal Artillery until 1946. After postwar overseas duty in the Foreign Office he joined the Monitoring Service of the BBC in 1950, rising through External Broadcasting to become Controller of Administration in 1975 and retiring from the BBC in 1980.

A man with a deep feeling for his countrymen and a healthy disregard for the voice of authority, Lance Thirkell has interested himself in local Government, adventure playgrounds, ex-prisoner welfare and youth projects. He is married, with four children and is President of the Angela Thirkell Society.

∞∞∞∞∞∞∞∞∞∞∞∞∞∞∞

About a year ago I had a presentiment, unspecified, that something nasty was about to happen, and did all the usual things like tidying up my affairs, making wills and getting everything as straight as possible. I hadn't the least idea of what it was but, after a long period of tiredness and tetchiness I was suddenly discovered by my family to be bright yellow in the face and even worse in the temper, and in fact I had a very severe attack of jaundice.

After tests at my local hospital I was admitted to the

Wellington, where I had a major operation which was, in effect, a complete re-plumbing of my stomach. This was followed by two more operations, a spell in a nursing home to recuperate and since then a further series of tests for suspected cancer. Each negative test meant one more day – or one more week – to live and not to become a cabbage or an object of sympathy. It was finally decided that further drastic treatments would not be advisable and that I must rely henceforth on a programme of drugs and drops. I am now a mobile dispensary with, as one consultant observed, no right, medically, to be alive.

At this stage I would like to make a number of observations concerning my time in the hospital and the nursing home. Firstly, I am convinced that one nurse can provide as much spiritual encouragement as a dozen clergymen. The gentleness, the kindness of those ladies is beyond belief; they were never soppy or sentimental, they made me do as I was told but they carried me for parts of the time. I went into my first operation, as I went into the D-day landing, full of fight and adrenalin and fought the damn thing every inch of the way. When we came to the second I had just lost the will to resist and had no fight left in me. For forty-eight hours those little nurses fought for me with all their dedication and training, and at the end of that period they said, 'We have done our bit. It is now up to you whether you live or whether you die. Just get on with it.'

They have their soft side. One darling little junior sister, when I had been in just three days, stopped on her way off duty and looked over the edge of my cot to see that I was all right. As I was a little tired I pretended to be asleep. That child leant over my cot, took hold of my hand and gave me a kiss on the forehead. And although I am a grown man and an ex-soldier I nearly cried.

The nursing home was another glorious experience. They said, 'You've been in hospital. You are now very high, almost hysterical, you talk far too much and we are going to calm you down.' And, by God, they did! It was back to the nursery. 'You *would* like to finish your rice pudding and prunes, Mr Thirkell, wouldn't you?' 'You *would* like to go back to bed now, Mr Thirkell, wouldn't you?' But they achieved their objective and sent me off to my Suffolk cottage to convalesce.

From my experiences in the past year I have reached a few conclusions, one of which is the importance of maintaining a sense of humour throughout. You are in hospital not to be looked after but to entertain and amuse your nurses, because they get bored with patients who gripe and whinge and moan. The doctors seem to like it too, although surgical humour is a touch heavy at times: 'We broke the bed; it's a pity we didn't break the patient instead – they're cheaper to replace' – that kind of thing.

Conclusion number two is that if you are going to be really ill do please have a wife and family. In normal times they will drive you up the wall and across the ceiling, but when you are very, very ill they suddenly become involved. They rally to your side and nothing is too much trouble. They look after you, are kind to you, the children stop misbehaving and become adults. I would strongly recommend anybody ill to have a family.

The next one, I am quite clear, is a determination to get well. You can call it prayer, you can call it guts or anything you like. A lot of people did pray for me. I don't know whether it helped or not. There's no proof that it does and no proof that it doesn't. Nobody, after all, would have believed in wireless waves before they were discovered and maybe there is some sort of wave which does convey prayer. But every single person I have met, including many genuine cancer sufferers, have said – and I know it's true – that you can kill yourself in hospital if you want to. Just turn your face to the wall and die – or you can determine to fight the whole way and this lengthens the odds on your surviving and the time for which you will survive.

Also very importantly, try not to think of yourself the whole time, although your own future fate is frightening and absorbing, particularly in the small hours of the morning. Do think about the people around you – notice other patients, talk to them. They like it and it does take your mind off yourself.

And finally, for anybody who goes in for this sort of thing, try not to be afraid of pain. Today this can be controlled to a great extent, indeed a lot of so-called pain can be no more than discomfort, and if you can teach yourself to relax – yoga, Alexander technique, deep breathing, anything, you name it – it does help.

All I can say now is that I am a total fraud. I am still undiagnosed, I am certainly not well, I am certainly going to spend the rest of my life under observation, I am certainly going to have to rely on batteries of pills, vitamins and the rest. I may well have a malignant cancer, on the other hand the trouble may well clear up. I now view the whole matter with an idle curiosity and am beginning to learn to live from day to day and from week to week.

Wendy Toye

Theatrical producer, film director, choreographer, actress, dancer. In her long and distinguished career, which started at the age of twelve at the Old Vic, Wendy Toye was a member of Ninette de Valois' original Vic Wells Ballet, toured with Anton Dolin's and Alicia Markova's ballet company and arranged dances and ballets for many shows and films. The theatrical productions which she has either directed or choreographed number far too many to mention here, but they cover presentations in London, Edinburgh, Chichester, Manchester, Monte Carlo, Canada, Paris, Turkey, Denmark and Latin America. She was awarded the Silver Jubilee Medal in 1977.

The incident she has described for us is one which she modestly plays down, but to those who have been the victims of such attacks the recovery can be long and difficult.

∞∞∞∞∞∞∞∞∞∞∞∞∞∞∞

Taken in the whole context of one's life, my story is of a very minor incident, but one which, nevertheless, left a scar which had to be eradicated. I was mugged in my own home.

I had a flat in Maddox Street in the West End of London at the time, the two top floors of the building, with my own front door. It was seven o'clock in the evening and I was expecting a very dear friend to dinner. There I was, in the kitchen, with my apron on and engrossed in my cooking. The doorbell rang. Thinking it must be my guest, I went down, opened the door and leant out to greet him. Instead there were two men, with handkerchiefs tied over their faces. One of them grabbed me by the throat, hit me quite a lot and finally pushed me down the stairs in a heap. Then they grabbed me again, holding my hands behind my back and forced me back into the flat and into the nearest room. They demanded to know where my valuables were kept and when I didn't answer they started to hit me again in the face. The absurdity of the situation was that, now gagged and blindfolded, I was quite unable to talk anyway. What my eventual fate would have been I can only guess, as Providence came to my rescue in an unexpected way.

One of the men, who appeared to be in charge, was anxious to get on and away with my goods. The other, however, was drunk and was more interested in trying to rip off my clothes, which held up progress. Now although that was most unpleasant and frightening I think it was my salvation, because the other man – the boss – pulled him away and continued questioning me. Still, of course, no coherent replies from me through my gag. So they then started stabbing my eyes with a pointed instrument to try and make me talk. I later found they were using the three-pin plug from the lead of my electric fire. I struggled violently and the boss man then snarled, 'If you scratch me I'll pull your fingernails out.' He then held me down while the other searched the room. They then trussed me up like a chicken with the lead from the electric fire, so that they could both ransack the remaining rooms of the flat. At this point I knew instinctively that they did not intend to kill me. My gag had worked loose and I became quite calm and told them, 'I don't know what you expect to find. I have nothing of value. But I will tell you something, I think you had better be quick and not stay much longer as I have some friends arriving for dinner shortly and you will be in trouble. So as soon as the street doorbell goes I advise you to leave at once.' Feverishly they left me, still trussed up, and rushed upstairs, where I heard them turning out all my drawers. Still blindfolded, but determined now to press my advantage, I started to yell for help as loudly as I could. I can only assume that by this time they were both disappointed and demoralized, for before long they rushed downstairs again, past my room door and out of the flat. I finally managed to free myself and with the help of my next-door neighbour the police were called. They arrived to find me with my clothes torn, my face bruised, one tooth loose, bloody but unbowed.

This incident happened around 1955–56, when I was directing the film *True as a Turtle* with Cecil Parker, John Gregson, Keith Michell and a number of other good colleagues. The next thing I knew was when members of the cast turned up at the flat armed with every security device possible: chains, bolts, alarms, bells. This did much for my morale, and the day after the mugging I went down to the studio and continued filming.

There were, of course, reactions. You don't endure an experience like that and get away scot free.

When I was in the street I was constantly looking behind me. Although not really scared I was on edge all the time, and this went on for ages. It was the uncanny feeling of being followed, and indeed, when the case came to court (for the men had been arrested) and I had to attend, I was followed on my way to the court by a strange car and the police had warned me this might happen.

It was a long time before I could bring myself to talk about the experience. I don't know what it is that directs these matters, but you seem to lose confidence for a while and then you get it back again, because you believe in the good rather than the evil in life.

Finally I believe you gain untold strength through discipline in youth. For instance from the age of five until I was eighteen – probably twenty – I don't think a single day passed without my doing an hour's class or practice, even when I was on holiday. It did wonders for me, and such injuries as I have had since then I have overcome through the mental and physical strength I gathered when I was young.

Nigel Tranter OBE

Nigel Tranter is one of the most prolific writers of his generation. Apart from the many books on Scotland for which he is uniquely famous, he has written no less than sixty-four novels, including twelve for children.

Educated at George Heriot's School, Edinburgh, he trained in accountancy and served in the RASC and the RA during the 1939-45 war, before becoming a full-time writer.

Always actively interested in Scottish public affairs, he has chaired a number of Scottish organizations and committees and has contributed to many journals on Scots history, genealogy and architecture.

Nigel Tranter was born in 1909, married in 1933 and enjoyed a happy partnership for forty-six years.

∞∞∞∞∞∞∞∞∞∞∞∞∞∞∞

It happened on 19 August 1966, without any sort of warning. A policeman came to our door and announced, with some embarrassment, that our son had been killed in a car crash in France.

Philip, our only son, was then aged twenty-seven. He had lived an adventurous life which, I must admit, had given my wife and myself many an anxious moment. He was a civil engineer by profession but by inclination he was a mountaineer and rock-climber, and had been since boyhood. He had founded a mountaineering club in Scotland, pioneered some very difficult climbs, and had been the first to climb all the Munroes in Scotland (that is, the mountains over 3,000 feet in height, over 540 of them) twice; and only the year before he had been one of the four-man Scottish Hindu Kush Expedition of 1965, which had climbed nineteen hitherto unclimbed mountains in Afghanistan over 20,000 feet, Philip himself giving them names, after peaks they resembled, at least in outline, in Scotland, names which were later accepted by the Afghan authorities. The four had taken many risks in that expedition, including driving to Afghanistan and back in an old Land Rover, but to our great relief had all returned in safety. Then, this next year, he and two friends had gone off on a lesser climbing adventure in the Caucasus Mountains, including the ascent of Mount Elbruz and Mount Ararat. It was on the return journey from this, with Philip asleep in the back of his car, one of his friends driving presumably dozed off at the wheel and crashed into a roadside tree in the North of France. Philip was killed, the only one.

To say that my wife and I were stricken is to put it mildly. Apart from the shattering loss, it seemed scarcely credible and so pointless, that one who had done so much in his short life and faced so many hazards, should have lost it in such circumstances. It all took a deal of accepting – even though we both had sufficient faith to recognize that it was only a question of time until we caught up with Philip again, in a better place than this.

But meantime we had to face the pain and loss. After a dire few days, awaiting the body being flown home by the French authorities and the arrival of his belongings and climbing diaries, written up until the night before, plus getting through the funeral, we came to certain conclusions. Somehow we had to get on top of this grief. We would never lose it, but we must not lose ourselves in its misery, and in the questioning why, why? Philip had had so much to look forward to, so much that he was going to do with his life, quite apart from mountaineering and exploring. To do – that was the point. We had to do something about it all – Philip would be expecting that. So we came to a conclusion. We would do something, and do it together, as a sort of therapy and a memorial, at least in our own minds.

A writer like myself lives very much inside his own head, dependent on himself for the daily production of his material, his words, ideas, stories. My publishers had more than once suggested that I write a kind of Scottish successor to the *King's England* series of books, which describes parish by parish the English counties and countryside. I had always rejected this, as too time-consuming, bound to interfere with my production of novels (which was my daily bread) with all the travel and research, the visiting of every parish in Scotland, and the describing in depth and detail every item of interest in each, ancient and modern. But now, here was something which we could do together, which would keep us both very busy, travelling the land, exploring its every feature, digging out the material, the history, the things to see, investigating, noting, describing. My wife would do it all with me, map-reading for me as we drove, taking notes, interviewing people, asking directions, and so on, even if it was myself who ultimately wrote it all down in words. She would do the indexing too, a mighty task, with thousands of items to record. We would make the *Queen's Scotland* series together.

And we did, four large volumes, dealing with literally hundreds of parishes. It took us a long time, ten years in fact, with the first volume published in 1971 and the fourth in 1977. The series was never finished, sadly, for my wife died thereafter and I had not the heart to continue it alone, for it had become so very mutual a task. But it was worth the doing, we felt, and we ourselves learned so much and may have passed on to others something which may have been of some value. And Philip would be approving.

So now I have two of them waiting for me somewhere. I wonder what our next joint venture will be?

Baroness Trumpington

The daughter of the late Major Campbell-Harris MC, she was educated privately in England and France. After two years at the outset of the war in 1939 as landgirl to Lloyd George at Churt, she spent the remainder of the war years in Naval Intelligence at Bletchley Park. The immediate postwar years were spent in assignments in London, Paris and New York until 1963, when she became a Cambridge City Councillor and Mayor of Cambridge in 1971-72. Raised to the peerage in 1980, she became a Baroness-in-Waiting and a Government spokesman for the Home Office and Commonwealth Office 1983-85 and was appointed Joint Parliamentary Undersecretary of State for Health and Social Security in 1985.

Married in 1954 to William Alan Barker, Headmaster of The Leys School, Cambridge, subsequently Headmaster of University College School, Hampstead, Lady Trumpington has one son. As Hon. Fellow of Lucy Cavendish College, Cambridge, she is President of the Association of Heads of Independent Schools and a Steward of Folkestone Racecourse.

∞∞∞∞∞∞∞∞∞∞∞∞∞∞∞

As November days go, the third of November 1981 started in the most promising kind of way. The sun shone, the air was crisp and it was the day of the State Opening of Parliament. My husband Alan had arranged a day away from University College School, Hampstead, of which he was Headmaster and we were intent on getting to Westminster in time to get seats with a good view of the proceedings.

We had planned the whole day with care. I had obtained a ticket in the Royal Gallery for a great friend with whom we were to meet up for lunch after the ceremony and we both had separate invitations for the remainder of the day. On our arrival at the House of Lords, we were separated, Alan up in the gallery with the Peeresses, I in the Chamber, dressed like my several hundred colleagues, all looking like so many Father Christmases.

After lunch I went back to the House of Lords to listen to the Humble Address before driving myself home to Hampstead to prepare for my evening engagement, a pleasant dinner party at the club of an old friend, to be followed by a game of bridge. Alan was to have dinner with a group of fellow Headmasters in a private room at the Public Schools Club, after an afternoon business meeting.

The time was 9.30 p.m. We had finished our meal and were all feeling full of good food, good wine and bonhomie – all was right with the world – when a waiter suddenly bent over me and whispered, 'There are two gentlemen here, who say they must see you.' I excused myself from the table and went outside, to be faced by two men who were perfect strangers to me, both looking very uncomfortable. 'We are terribly sorry,' said one, 'but Alan seems to have had a stroke. He has gone by ambulance to Westminster Hospital and we have come to take you there.' They were, it turned out, two of Alan's dinner party, fellow headmasters.

Alan lay on the examining bed in a small cubicle. I asked him how he felt. 'A splitting headache,' came the reply, in a perfectly normal voice, a voice – and appearance – that made me feel his illness could not be too bad. At last, around 2 a.m., he was moved upstairs into a ward and I was left, still unsuitably dressed in my evening gown, to go back alone to an empty house, carrying his clothes in a plastic bag. I learned next day that it had been a massive stroke. Alan was completely paralyzed, able only to move his right arm, and would have to spend the rest of his life, helpless in a wheelchair.

I was bemused. It seemed an extraordinary thing to be married, on one day, to somebody much fitter than yourself and on whom you have been able to rely, for thirty years, for support in so many ways, and then suddenly, the next day, to find your husband a totally dependent person – and dependent on you. Little things began to assume exaggerated importance, like the fact that our dog had to be handed over to another master at the school, like having to change a light bulb (never before in thirty years!) and it began to dawn on me that from now on, all the decisions, major and minor, would have to be made by me.

The situation was complicated by my husband's failure to realize his total dependency. The brain is a strange organ, and Alan's was well above average, but for a long time he refused to accept his position, which created a further anxiety for me. He stayed in the Westminster Hospital for three and a half months, and then went to the Wolfson Rehabilitation Centre, where he spent a further four months before coming home.

By that time I had had our house in Sandwich, on the Kent coast, altered to accommodate his needs. I could not have him back to the house in Hampstead. There were steps up to the front door, it was impossible to get a wheelchair into the bathroom – and, of course, when it became accepted that Alan could no longer expect to return to his job, we had to move out as the house was tied to the school.

Our little house in Sandwich was the only answer, but during the conversion I myself had nowhere to live and life was unfamiliar and strange. Alan's return home brought a fresh set of circumstances. Every weekend I went down to Sandwich and the marvellous girl who looked after him during the week went off, while I took over for the weekend. So it meant that, together with my job at Westminster during the week, I got very little rest indeed. One can carry on under pressure for only so long, but it is strange how fate can step in and redress the balance. In March 1986, four and a half years after his stroke, my husband became very ill and had to be moved from Sandwich as it had become impracticable to give him satisfactory daily support. As a disabled ex-soldier, wounded in the 1939–45 war, he was able to move into the Royal Star and Garter Home at Richmond-upon-Thames, where he remains and has the best possible professional attention and I am able to visit him at weekends, with time to talk and to listen.

The years since November 1981 have not been easy but I am certainly not sorry for myself. Inevitably there has been much on the credit side, things which sometimes only become apparent – or are only appreciated – against a background of tragedy. Among mine I number the great kindnesses shown to me by my friends and colleagues at Westminster. The House of Lords has been, and continues to be, a welcoming home and I have been made to feel part of a caring family. When one is neither a widow, a divorcee or single and is destined to attend parties and functions alone, the comfort of a 'safe refuge' cannot be over-emphasised.

Finally, I have been uniquely privileged in one particular way. As a Parliamentary Under-secretary of State for Health and Social Security I am the Minister responsible for war pensioners. This means that, in seeking to safeguard and promote their interests, I am personally equipped by experience to understand the special problems of wheelchair people – and indeed, the problems of those who have to look after them. It would appear that even the darkest cloud has a silver lining if one looks hard enough for it.

Ravenna Tucker

Born in Malaysia in 1962 and brought up in Hong Kong, Ravenna Tucker won the Adeline Genée Gold Medal competition in London at the age of sixteen. Accepted into the Royal Ballet Upper School, she was invited in her second year to join the Royal Ballet Company, with whom she is now a principal dancer.

By sheer dedication, hard work and single-minded application she overcame the problem of establishing a career in a European company from an initial school training in the Far East.

∞∞∞∞∞∞∞∞∞∞∞∞∞

I was born in Malaysia and when I was seven years of age we moved to Hong Kong. At that time I had no clear idea about a career in dancing, and anyway, in Malaysia it would not have been possible. But I was, even at that age, very active. My father ran the Outward Bound school in Hong Kong, and I used to go out sailing, canoeing, swimming and rock climbing. I grew very strong and athletic and I loved all sports.

Soon after I enrolled at my new school a circular came round inviting pupils to attend ballet classes after school on Friday afternoons. I knew I would like dancing and that was how I started. I enjoyed it very much indeed and worked very hard at it, going through the grades from one up to preparation for the Royal Academy of Dancing exams. When I was eleven I went up on points and then the work began to get more difficult, more exacting and more demanding. But at the same time it became more and more interesting and there was no way I could stop. Needless to say I didn't want to stop, but the pace grew faster and more intense. From Friday afternoons it increased to two hours three times a week and when I was sixteen, doing my advanced work, it meant going every day for two or three hours after school.

At that time, of course, I was also studying hard for my 'O' Levels and it became a really hard time both for me and for my parents. We lived out in the country about an hour's drive from town, so it meant getting up at 7 a.m. leaving at 8, school from 9 until 4 in the afternoon, and then on to ballet from 5 until 7 o'clock, getting home at 8, doing my homework for 'O' Levels and rarely getting to bed before 10 o'clock.

There was absolutely no relaxation. Even at break times at school I would start on my homework in order to get some of it done before evening, and this would go on, day after day, week in week out, without a break.

But I had already decided, at the age of fifteen, that I wanted to be a dancer and from then on I was absolutely single-minded about it. However, living out in Hong Kong, I had no idea at all how to go about it. There were certainly no opportunities out there. So I read every book I could find on ballet and learned what was happening in other countries. I learned about the Royal Ballet in England, the Bolshoi in Moscow, the American ballet companies and I got to know a lot of the names of the leading dancers and choreographers but I never knew, nor could I imagine, that I would one day be part of it all myself. I did know, though, that the Upper School of the Royal Ballet School took pupils at the age of sixteen and if I could find some way to get into it, to consolidate all I had learned in Hong Kong, I might be able to go to auditions with a view to getting into a ballet company.

Fortunately I did quite well in my intermediate ballet exam in Hong Kong and the Honours Grade entitled me to enter a competition in England known as the Adeline Genée Gold

Medal Ballet Competition. This was the first time ever that a Hong Kong student had qualified for it and everyone was delighted and determined that I should go to England and enter. All the parents clubbed together to finance the trip for myself and two other girls who were also going from two other ballet schools. We came over, rehearsed and did the competition, which took place at the Sadler's Wells Theatre. There were fifteen competitors and I won it. That entitled me to a gold medal, £100 and a place at the Royal Ballet School. This was not a scholarship, but a guaranteed place if one wanted to go there.

Strangely enough, before I was given the chance to enter the competition I applied to go to the Royal Ballet School, backed up by exam results, recommendations and everything I could possibly muster up to support my application. I had been accepted, so winning the Adeline Genée competition guaranteed my entrance to the school without any doubt.

That summer I went back to Hong Kong to take my 'O' Levels and after the summer holiday I flew back to England again to start my first term at the Royal Ballet School. Being there was wonderful, a new found freedom and the opportunity to concentrate on dancing all the time. The company was housed in the same building and it was a thrill to be able to watch them at work.

I was at the school for a year and at the start of my second year, that was in October 1979, they asked me if I would like to join the company. I was so thrilled, I could not believe my luck. I had been planning in my mind, that in the following summer I would go around Europe, auditioning, never thinking for one moment I might get into the Royal Ballet Company itself. Out of a form of thirty girls it is usual for two or three to be taken into the company each year and another two or three into the sister company at Sadler's Wells. So it was a great honour and, to me, unbelievable.

I have been with the company ever since and am now a principal dancer with them, but I still have a long way to go and plenty to learn. There are always new roles to learn and new tours for which to prepare. This year we are going to Japan and Korea for a month, then back for a month and then off to Russia for a month, dancing in Leningrad, Moscow and Odessa.

I was once asked by a reporter what advice I would give to a young dancer with ambition. There is only one true answer and that is, 'Work, work, work.' The old saying is so true – 'one per cent inspiration, ninety-nine per cent perspiration.'

Charles Vance

Charles Vance was educated at Queens University, Belfast and began his acting career when he was twenty at the Gate Theatre, Dublin. In 1985 he celebrated twenty-five years as an Actor/Manager, having formed his company in 1960 with his actress/director wife Imogen Moynihan. A year later, he founded the Civic Theatre in Chelmsford and subsequently for six years was actor/manager of the Eastbourne Theatre Company.

In 1976 he took over the Leas Pavillion Theatre in Folkestone which he ran until 1985 before taking over control of the Beck Theatre in London in 1986. His numerous acting credits include 'Sir Thomas More' in *A Man for all Seasons*, 'Archie Rice' in *The Entertainer* and 'Maxim de Winter' in *Rebecca*.

Prominent in the world of theatre politics, he currently serves as Chairman of the Government's Standing Advisory Committee on Local Authority and the Theatre, and as Vice-Chairman of the Theatre's Advisory Council. He was, for several years, President of the Theatrical Management Association and he serves on many other theatre governing bodies.

Outside the theatre his interests include cooking (he is a *Cordon Bleu* chef), sailing and travel. He is a Barker of the Variety Club of Great Britain, a Fellow of the Royal Society for the Arts, a Vice President of the RSPCA and a member of Rotary International.

In the following pages he describes two major crises in his life. To recover from the first he actually sailed single-handed across the Atlantic – accompanied only by a cat.

∽∽∽∽∽∽∽∽∽∽∽∽∽∽∽∽∽

'La peur; c'est l'inconnue.' So wrote Guy de Maupassant in his famous essay *La Peur*. And so it was that when faced with a fear, one realized that it was the unknown that one was fearing and not something physical.

It was in the mid-1950s and the world appeared to have collapsed. The unexpected temporary demise, yet again, of the British film industry had seen the end of my magical contract and within a matter of days I had discovered that my unhappy alcoholic wife was beyond rescue. I fled. I fled professionally to France where I was fortunate to be given the opportunity of making a film on the south coast while I tried to recover the tattered remnants of my emotional chaos. My tempestuous marriage had had little to commend it but, none the less, it was an intense and very committed relationship and although the steps I had taken were to relieve me from the pressures of dealing with an alcoholic, at which I was so inadequate, something more frightening was to take its place. I was afraid. I was afraid of loneliness. We all know the feeling in a crowded room at a party or a gallery or wherever and the realization that one is totally alone. But this was a different type of solitude. This was a loneliness of emotion, a loneliness within which there was no sharing of one's problems or of one's thoughts.

I was brought up in a simple philosophy. The one way to fight something of which you are afraid is to face it head on and after all, Maupassant had said, 'fear is the unknown'.

The child is afraid of the dark, not because the dark itself is frightening but because of what it might contain. Switch the light on and the fear is removed. The other side of the locked door in the somewhat eerie house can be frightening but once we open that door and see what is on the other side, no matter how great the challenge that may lie there, it is something we can physically handle because we are aware of its entity.

And so there was one inevitable task – I had to face the ultimate physical loneliness. I had always loved the sea and as a child had sailed a dinghy in my native waters of Northern Ireland. I finished my filming and with the rewards of my efforts bought a small sailing craft which I prepared for crossing the Atlantic – alone! This was no sense of bravado. I did not seek any sense of achievement or heroics – I loved the sea and I could think of no other place where I could face up to the hazards of loneliness than the middle of the Atlantic ocean. Three months after making the decision – three months of arduous effort in preparing the boat, equipping it and making it seaworthy – I set sail. The first days were still within what we might term coastal waters: sailing through the Mediterranean to Gibraltar, to Tangier, to the Canary Islands before hazardously setting off south-west into the Atlantic to meet the Trade Winds to carry me to the Caribbean. I had sail but no engine; I had books but no wireless; I had a pussy cat but no human crew.

The ocean made its demands of the little ship and its erstwhile sailor. I was visited almost daily by dolphins and other wondrous creatures of the sea. I faced rough seas and if not tempests, I faced high winds and, after thirty-two days of an exciting and adventurous voyage, I made a landfall in St Lucia in the Caribbean.

This is not meant to be a story of the achievement of a sailor – this is a very simple statement of a lonely man who discovered in the middle of the Atlantic Ocean that there was no such thing as loneliness. Whether our God be the Christian Almighty or the Allah of the Mohammedan or to me, a Jew, the Lord Our God of Israel, is irrelevant; what is important is that one man can meet his God when he believes himself to be alone and suddenly discovers a companionship which he cannot find among his fellow men. That was my first experience of winning through.

Fifteen years later when my second wife and I were running our theatre companies all over the country, I had been privileged to be elected President of the governing body of my profession and we had some five or six repertory companies and touring companies functioning at the same time, the world was exciting and indeed was our oyster – we were hurtling towards the pinnacle of our career. Our daughter was eight years old and at prep. school. We were resident at the Devonshire Park Theatre at Eastbourne; my wife was directing in the theatre at Torquay; we were planning our season in Malvern, Whitby and other towns and I was not only directing a play in Tunbridge Wells but appearing in another one at night in Eastbourne. We had a partner – he was our Financial Controller. As I walked into rehearsal on a certain Thursday morning, a package was brought to me by a messenger. It contained the company's cheque book and a note from our erstwhile partner saying, 'Goodbye. Good luck for the future.' Rehearsals had to go on; the play's the thing and that came first. Within twenty-four hours we discovered that there was nothing in the bank; we didn't know what bills had been paid and what hadn't. I was the President of the governing body and didn't know how I would pay next week's wages and I feared for my pride. I wrote a letter to every single supplier for our theatre company; I wrote a letter to every single actor and every single one of them without exception rallied round. This had nothing to do with financial victories – this was the warmth of fellow men supporting their colleague at a time of crisis without question to enable him to survive. No one in the profession questioned what we had to do. I spoke to the managers of the theatres where we would play and they arranged that we should have advance payments for our productions and so the show went on and the company survived.

In that amazing experience which involved some fifty or sixty of my colleagues, I learned perhaps the most important word of all – humility – and at the same time an understanding of the strength that can be given to one in trouble by the woman who stands by your side, for never once did my wife question what had to be done, indeed, she was the guiding force of getting ahead and doing it.

And so in these two illustrations of winning through, I found perhaps the two most important things in our lives. On that little boat in the 1950s I learned that there were more things in heaven than on earth and, fifteen years later, I learned of the generosity of my fellow men.

I am very privileged to have been allowed two opportunities of 'winning through'.

Ian Wallace OBE

One of our most celebrated and well-loved actor singers, Ian Wallace was educated at Charterhouse and Trinity Hall, Cambridge, where he obtained an MA degree. After serving in the Royal Artillery in the 1939–45 war, he made his London stage debut at Sadler's Wells in 1945 and the following year commenced his prodigious singing career, which has embraced the field of opera from Mozart, Verdi and Rossini to the light opera of Gilbert and Sullivan and covered seasons with the New London Opera Company, Scottish Opera, Glyndebourne and the Welsh National Opera.

Television and radio have also been enriched by his regular involvement over the past twenty years and his closing songs in the *My Music* series continue to enchant viewers and listeners everywhere.

There can be few musical performers of this stature who can exceed Ian Wallace's tireless programme. Small wonder that he has found material for two autobiographies. Among his recreations he lists, 'singing a song about a hippopotamus to children of all ages,' and we, his fans, hope he will never tire of doing so.

∞∞∞∞∞∞∞∞∞∞∞∞∞∞

In October 1942 there were quite a few places, especially in North Africa, where a second lieutenant, Royal Artillery, might find himself in a hazardous situation. Mine, however, turned out to be much nearer home. On a sunny late autumn morning in that year I walked painfully into the clinic room of a Surrey hospital to meet for the first time Hubert Wood, an orthopaedic surgeon of considerable reputation. Quietly he told me that there was no doubt that I had tuberculosis of the spine and that it would be necessary to immobilize me in a plaster cast for a long period with the possibility of major surgery over and above.

Before leaving this tall, thin, pale-faced man in his white coat, attended by a couple of younger doctors and the ample figure of the ward sister, I nerved myself to ask the question that an elderly man might have preferred to leave unanswered. 'What are my chances of getting better?' He thought for a minute and then handed me one of the x-ray pictures. I held it up to the sun coming through the window and incongruously remembered being given a negative at school through which to look at an eclipse of the sun.

'You'll notice that those two vertebrae in the lumbar region look a bit like decayed teeth. Well, unlike teeth, it's possible for calcium to form and protect them from further decay, but I'm bound to say that the odds are no better than fifty-fifty.'

I was twenty-two, single and it was the middle of a world war. The odds, compared with those facing many of my friends flying sorties with the RAF or sailing with convoys to Russia, seemed acceptable. All the more so as I had won a previous battle with the tubercle bacillus two years earlier when it had attacked what can be delicately described as my genito-urinary system. After two frighteningly intimate operations I was pronounced cured though there was a reservation. I could still call myself an eligible bachelor but I was unlikely to become a father.

It would be totally unfair to blame my father for any of this, though he was indirectly responsible for what happened. He had married late in life, having started work at fourteen in a linoleum works in Scotland. By sheer ability and hard work he rose to be its managing director in London. He was also, between the wars, a respected member of the House of

Commons. I, his only child, was born when he was fifty-one. By the sweat of his brow he was able to give me the sort of education he would have loved to have had himself and he fondly hoped that I would fulfil another of his unrealized ambitions and be called to the Bar.

Thus I went to read law at Trinity Hall, Cambridge, where I was when war broke out. In between the end of our examinations in 1940 and being embodied in the army, a number of us stayed in Cambridge with the cadet force and helped out the local troops with guard duties at strategic points like airfields. We lived in tents in daily expectation of an airborne invasion. Our milk supply came, still warm, from a nearby farm. The type of TB I contracted was identified as bovine. So if my poor old dad had sent me somewhere else – who knows? I might have been killed in action instead of being infected by milk from an untested cow.

I lay in that plaster cast for twenty months. Every three months there were new x-rays and new speculation about doing a big graft from my thigh bone into my spine. One by one the other patients with the same complaint died. Ironically they were some of the last to do so because drugs to treat the disease were discovered a year or two after I left hospital.

Whilst I lay on my back, able to read and converse with my fellow patients, many of whom were recovering from wounds or accidents (it was not a sanatorium) I had much time to reflect on what I would do if the even money bet on my recovery was a winner. My heart had never been in the law. I had scraped an honours degree of lowly status largely to please my father, but from the age of eight I had wanted to stand up and sing or recite the humorous monologues made so popular by Stanley Holloway. At school, at university or in the army I had gravitated towards any dramatic society or concert party that would have me.

Now I began to wonder, as the pains receded and I started to feel well in myself, whether there was not some purpose behind all the suffering I had endured, which had followed a childhood and boyhood where I had lacked for nothing and where I had been sheltered and very privileged. Though not much of a church-goer, I belong to the Christian faith in its simplest form.

As the days and months went past cocooned in hospital routine, I became more and more convinced that if I was going to recover it was because I was intended to devote my life to some sort of special service to my fellow man. I was equally convinced that it would be nothing to do with a legal career.

Call that wishful thinking if you like, but one day I suddenly felt a strong urge to try to write a musical play to be performed in the hospital. I had never done such a thing before. It was eventually performed and I directed it from my spinal carriage – something else I had never done before – even standing on my feet! Were you to go through the files of the *Daily Mirror* and find the edition for 21 January 1944, you'd realize that the show, entitled *High Temperature*, made quite an impact.

I emerged from that hospital cured, at least five stones overweight and convinced that I had found my vocation. Incidentally I never had to have the threatened operation, much to the disappointment of Mr Wood's young registrar who wanted the chance to see a great surgeon perform something that was a rarity in those days. I could not share his disappointment!

Sidney Weighell

Sidney Weighell is one of the most interesting and important characters in modern trade union history. Always his own man, he has conducted his professional life strictly in accordance with his own expressed principles and has earned the respect and affection of people on all sides of the political and industrial scene.

Born in 1922, he has spent most of his working life within the National Union of Railwaymen and as their General Secretary from 1975–83, during which time he was also a member of the TUC Council.

He is currently a director of BAA plc (which owns and operates seven major airports in Britain) and a Member and Governor of the Ditchley Foundation, an organization created to promote the joint study of, and education in, matters of common interest to the British and American peoples.

∞∞∞∞∞∞∞∞∞∞∞∞∞∞∞

On 20 December 1956 I was a happily married man of thirty-four years of age, with a loving wife and two small children. I was established as a full-time divisional officer of the National Union of Railwaymen and we were living comfortably in St Albans. Within twenty-four hours two of my loved ones were dead and the life we had built together was no more.

We were driving up the A1 on our way to spend Christmas with my wife's parents, who lived outside Northallerton. On the brow of a railway bridge just north of Newark a car driving south overtook and crashed head-on into us. I knew no more until Christmas Eve, when I regained consciousness in hospital in Sheffield. I could remember nothing of what had happened since leaving home, but I discovered that my jaws were wired together, I was unable to speak and I was in a hospital bed. My fears were confirmed when a nurse told me that my wife Margaret and six-year-old daughter Jenifer had been killed in the car accident. Anthony, our two-year-old son, had mercifully been saved by his harness and I had escaped with my jaw broken in two places and minor injuries to my ribs and legs.

After three months in hospital I went to convalesce for a while with my parents in Northallerton, but I found I could not cope with the well-meant sympathy of friends and neighbours, so I sought refuge with my wife's parents. They had a poultry farm in the quiet countryside five miles outside Northallerton and Anthony had been in their care since the accident.

It was there that I began to recognize that I had a responsibility to pick up the pieces and rebuild my life. I was still a relatively young man, with a son to bring up and I must face the world. Until then I had been too preoccupied with my own state, but getting to know my son again in those relaxed surroundings, trout fishing, walking on the moors and working on the farm, I knew I must make a new life for the benefit of both of us. I returned to Northallerton, took up golf, moved among the local people once again and began to work my way back into my Union job. The rest of my career is history and I can now look back on that traumatic period and analyze my recovery.

The greatest difficulty was the mental readjustment. It took me quite five years before I recovered, but I doubt if you ever recover fully. The first hurdle to overcome was meeting, in the Coroner's court, the man who had caused the accident and who was subsequently charged with dangerous driving. This was the man who was responsible for the loss of my wife and daughter, but I was also aware that he, too, had lost his wife and the unborn child she was carrying. As if this court encounter were not enough, I had to attend a further civil court dealing with the claim for damages and on each occasion I had to take part in the repetition of all the details of the crash.

The next problem to be tackled was the gaining of confidence to begin driving again. In this my father was a great help, but it took some time for me to feel at ease driving on my own, and even now I get worried if my second wife Joan or my son are travelling without me and are late in arriving.

During this period fate seemed both to help and to hinder at the same time. A big plus was having my Union job and the help and encouragement of Jim Campbell, the General Secretary. On the other side of the coin I began to suffer a loss of memory which, if not conquered, could easily put my job in jeopardy. My work entailed attending a variety of meetings, together with accident enquiries and all required the detailed knowledge for answering questions and a good memory was essential. Suffice it to say I survived, but another blow was on the way. Late in 1957 my good friend and superior officer, Jim Campbell, was killed in a car crash on a visit to the Soviet Union.

By now I was struggling to win through. My job took me travelling all over the country and I literally buried myself in it. I knew Anthony was in good hands, living with his grandparents, and I could visit him frequently at weekends, so I was free to concentrate on my work and this was a lifesaver.

Then in 1959 I had my greatest piece of good fortune. I found my second wife, who proved to be a wonderful support. Over the years, not only did she learn about the Labour and the trade union movements; she also protected the privacy of our off-duty home life and enabled us to form a united family again at last. Anthony grew up with no ill-effects, took an Honours degree at Keele University and later achieved his PhD at Aberystwyth.

It has been shown to me that it is possible to survive and to overcome a major family tragedy and I have written my personal story in the hope that it may bring hope and encouragement to the many people and families who are the victims of this kind of tragedy, so common in today's society. But nothing can be achieved without determination and effort, together with certain other ingredients. The first is faith – faith in the ultimate justice, which comes from a religious upbringing. I come from a Baptist family, brought up with strong beliefs and the faith which they bring. I think we all know that, even if we are not regular worshippers, we believe in a guiding spirit to whom we can turn in times of adversity. Secondly, we need the united family, who stand together and give mutual support in times of trouble, and thirdly, good friends and a fair slice of luck. Given these factors, together with the will to put the past behind you and build afresh from what still remains to you, I believe there is always hope, however dark the clouds may seem.

Finally, my personal tragedy has taught me to look at life's ups and downs in true perspective. After overcoming my problems I am able to make a reasoned assessment of the more minor frustrations and disappointments of everyday life and to rise above them.

Air Chief Marshal Sir Neil Wheeler GCB CBE DSO DFC AFC

Educated at St Helens College, Southsea, Sir Neil Wheeler entered the Royal Air Force College, Cranwell in 1935. He served in Bomber Command from 1937-40 and in Fighter and Coastal Commands throughout the Second World War, after which he held progressive appointments in the Air Ministry, the RAF College and the Ministry of Defence.

Sir Neil served as ADC to Her Majesty the Queen from 1957-61, and was Senior Air Staff Officer, HQ RAF Germany (2nd TAF) from 1963-66. After commanding FEAF in 1969-70 he held further senior appointments until 1977, when he became a Director of Rolls-Royce Limited.

Sir Neil is a member of the Council of the Air League and was Master of the Guild of Air Pilots and Air Navigators in 1986-87. He is married and has two sons and one daughter.

∞∞∞∞∞∞∞∞∞∞∞∞∞∞

I have frequently been accused of being a pessimist. I would prefer to say that I always endeavour to see the possible pitfalls before I embark on any course of action. Indeed, my navigator/wireless operator with whom I did most of my Beaufighter flying during 1942-43, many years later said, 'I thought you took incredible risks when we were flying together but I was always confident you had previously thought out an escape route.' It therefore gives me some satisfaction to recount an episode in my life when optimism, or at any rate apparent optimism, and tenacity were essential.

In the autumn of 1942, after a rest period from operations, I was posted to a Coastal Command Beaufighter operational training unit in Yorkshire. At the time I was a Squadron Leader of twenty-five and, after only about ten days, the Station Commander sent for me and told me to put up the stripes of a Wing Commander and proceed forthwith to command a Beaufighter Squadron in Lincolnshire. He warned me that I must expect morale to be poor in the Squadron because they had taken part in a Wing attack on shipping off the coast of Holland when not only the Squadron Commander, my predecessor, but also a number of other air crew had not returned. Alas, his forecast was only too true – morale was rock bottom.

Three Squadrons of Beaufighters, two armed with guns and bombs, and the third with guns and torpedoes, had been brought together as a Wing to attack shipping convoys off the Dutch coast. To do this in an area with a heavy concentration of German fighter aircraft made it essential to have a fighter escort. In spite of escort being arranged, on the first big attack led by my predecessor, no rendezvous took place and the Beaufighters attacked on their own. The anti-aircraft fire of the ships was devastating enough without added havoc from enemy fighters.

On taking over command of the squadron I found my two Squadron Leaders ten years older than me with many flying hours, mostly as civil flying instructors, to their credit. However, they were always completely loyal to me and I had the advantage of some two years' operational experience. The rest of the crews were very young men, as I was, but they had only joined up for the war. Added to their poor morale was their sense of failure that the Squadron had not achieved what was expected of it. None the less, my first impression was that the majority were keen, able and courageous aircrew and I was determined not to be proved wrong.

The Station Commander, on the other hand, was an unfortunate choice for an operational station. Although an excellent flying instructor in his day, he never flew a Beaufighter and never flew on operations. A great worrier, I found him no support and it was a relief when he was replaced after a few months. Of the other two Squadron Commanders in the Wing, one was a brave torpedo pilot but was totally pessimistic about future operations, the other was a sick man, so both had to be replaced. Sadly, the two new Squadron Commanders were lost on operations within six months. It will thus be realized that I felt very much alone and without senior support. I realized that it had been decided at Coastal Command HQ that, if any more disasters like the previous one took place, the whole concept of a Wing attack would be scrapped.

The reader will readily appreciate that my first few months with the Squadron were not easy or happy. However, I was young, pleased with the job and the promotion it brought, and very determined to succeed. I realized from the first that I was being closely watched by my aircrew. The essence of leadership is often said to be 'example' and I felt it certainly was then. It was imperative that, whatever my misgivings, they must not be apparent and I must appear confident and optimistic at all times. Put another way, I had always to show enthusiasm; and enthusiasm can, I discovered, be infectious. I set about an intense programme of armament training, formation flying, and a detailed study of tactics. Moreover, I made it absolutely clear to my Squadron that we would not operate without fighter escort. Added to which I would not be prepared to lead the Wing on operations until I was confident we were ready and capable of success.

Gradually I detected confidence and morale returning, added to a determination to succeed. The great day came early in 1943 and I set out leading the Wing with an escort of Spitfires. The attack was an unqualified success and, on their return, the aircrew were jubilant for, apart from sinking and damaging enemy ships, we had suffered no casualties. Success breeds success and that day was the start of a most successful anti-shipping campaign. Naturally we had our casualties – sometimes heavy, but everybody felt we knew what we were about. We were doing it well and were making a valuable contribution to the war effort. I cannot say that I was always confident and optimistic during the training period, but to have appeared unsure would have undoubtedly led to another disaster. I felt at the time that I was facing the biggest challenge of my life. That I was successful was undoubtedly due to determination and optimism. In addition, of course, I always had, and demonstrated, complete faith in my Squadron.

Laurence Whistler CBE FRSL

Laurence Whistler is best known as an engraver on glass. His work includes goblets, etc. in point engraving and drill. He has engraved many church windows and has had exhibitions both here and in the USA. He is also a writer of distinction, being the first recipient of the King's Gold Medal for Poetry in 1935 and the Atlantic Award for Literature in 1945. His publications include collections of his poems, books on Sir John Vanburgh and on his late brother, the artist Rex Whistler, besides writings on glass engraving.

Educated at Stowe and Balliol College, Oxford, he served in the Rifle Brigade in the 1939–45 war. His first wife, Jill Furse, died in 1944 after five years of marriage and in the following narrative he comments on the acceptance of bereavement.

∽∽∽∽∽∽∽∽∽∽∽∽∽∽∽∽∽∽

What is one to do if some disaster occurs? Nobody can answer the question in this general form. We are born into the flux of time, subject to perpetual change and loss, and are intensely vulnerable at every moment of our lives, physically, mentally, spiritually. Disasters of innumerable kinds are always threatening and not infrequently met with, even if we set aside the one which is inescapable, separating us from those we love and from life itself.

But to keep this thought in the forefront of the mind would be to risk neurosis. Therefore we are wise to assume that it is otherwise, that no one we love will be killed in a plane crash, develop cancer, or suffer a personality change; that we ourselves will not go soft in the head, blind or bankrupt; that all is pretty well, or even very well, as indeed it may be.

But what when it happens – the particular catastrophe? To some, like Juliet, the task of living on becomes unendurable. Most do live on, out of obligation to others – children, parents, friends – or to the one who has died and would not wish it otherwise, or out of self-respect and a sheer refusal to give up.

The thoughts that follow here are concerned with a single type of catastrophe: the death of somebody intensely loved. Can anything be done in advance by two together to alleviate for one of them the pain of being suddenly alone? Where a child is involved the answer surely is no. Children have to learn that dying is a precondition of living – even for themselves, incredibly – but they have to view it as one which will only be applied far away in the unimaginable future; for their sense of security depends on this. But in grown-up love, as between husband and wife, lover and mistress, or in any very close relationship, something there is, small though it may seem, which can be done in advance, and which is worth the doing. How often must the one left behind have reflected, 'If only we had once, unflinchingly, thought out this possibility together. If only I could hear her say – him say – what she – what he – would wish me to do now, and to be now, as I move into this alien landscape of grief, without guidance! More than ever before I need our love for the task of going on without it.'

Unfortunately lovers do flinch from casting a strong shadow on their happiness by candidly confronting its inevitable end on earth. Yet if they have confronted it to any extent, to that extent their happiness, in retrospect, will seem already to have come to terms with death, and the task will seem one that has already been shared while there were two to share it. 'Love knew about this,' the solitary mind will then reflect. 'Love allowed for it – still does.'

Whatever precautions are taken, bereavement often enough

has the force of an explosion. And what can friends or acquaintances do in that case? Little enough. But there is one small thing they can do: which is – not cross the road or escape from the room, rather than confront the bereaved. The excuse we make to ourselves is that the bereaved 'only wants to be left alone.' The motive is embarrassment: not knowing what to say on the subject. Nothing need be said. All the sufferer needs from us may be customary friendliness, in which some extra warmth in a touch or look will seem, if sincere, like a benison – even while the railway time-table is being opened, or a joke about the County Planning Officer is being made.

But this is not central to the problem. One has to go on. So one has to accept. And how is acceptance to be learnt? One way to approach it is to discern a kind of equity in bereavement; where the joy lost is the measure of the pain, and the antidote to it. For the having of love must always be worth the losing of it when the loss is by separation, not by decay. If stronger solace than that is demanded, there is really no substitute for faith in a world beyond time, with its hope of recognition and reunion. This faith is not to be had for the wishing. Yet it evidently *is* to be had.

Phillip Whitehead

Phillip Whitehead, born in 1937, was educated at Lady Manners Grammar School, Bakewell and Exeter College, Oxford. President of the Oxford Union in 1961, he joined the BBC after leaving university and was a producer until 1967, when he joined Thames Television as Editor of *This Week* (1967-70). From 1970 to 1983 he sat as Labour Member of Parliament for Derby North, during which time he served on a number of committees and was Opposition Front Bench Spokesman on Education from 1981-83. A writer and broadcaster, Phillip Whitehead was presenter of the TV series *Credo* and a *Times* columnist (1983-85). He is now Chairman of the *New Statesman* and director of Goldcrest Films and an independent TV producer. He is married and has three children.

As an adopted child, Phillip Whitehead tells how he discovered his identity and recalls the fears and the agony of his adoptive mother.

∞∞∞∞∞∞∞∞∞∞∞∞∞∞

It wasn't much of a crisis. Nowadays there are professionals to counsel, handbooks to advise. Then there was much less. My parents had known each other since infancy. Their solemn faces, at six, stare out from the village school photograph of 1896; she pert with frustrated enquiry and fun, he pudgy and solemn, too early motherless. In the Great War my father had gone away to Flanders with the Army Service Corps, straight from leaving school. My mother fell in love with a Canadian who came to fell our Derbyshire woods for the war effort. After it ended and his regiment went home, he lingered. Her brothers came home from the war, and took against him. She cried when she told how they tore up the photograph he left behind. I do not know when or why he went, but he took her youth and her high hopes with him. She stayed in our village, nursed an invalid mother, while her brothers returned to the Midland Railway.

Eventually her mother died. There were not many young men in the village; fewer still from that generation who now marched each November to stand by the cross in the village churchyard, where those who would not grow old were graven in stone. But there was my father, the wheelwright, from a family old in the village. Each generation they married later, as their blood ran thinner. He was a good man. She had always known him. They came together in the comfort of early middle age.

They were fifty when I arrived. It was no miracle of gynaecology, but a third-party adoption. Down the valley a sixteen-year-old schoolgirl had given birth. For a while her family kept her child, but she had an infant sister too, youngest of seven. The unexpected baby had to go out into the world. But not too far. As the law then allowed, there was a system of third-party adoption. A cousin was the intermediary. The cousin had a childless sister-in-law. And so my mother came to cope with nappies at fifty. It was not all she had to cope with. There had been no counselling, no support service. My mother (as I always think of her, more than that frightened schoolgirl who pined for her lost baby) conceived a great fear. One day 'they', the hardly-known middle class family four miles down the valley, would claim the baby back.

And so there was a tension, in the war and after, which had nothing to do with the thump of the bombs over Sheffield as we sat in our cellar, or the flashes of temper in dreary, weary queues. Even in a small village war brings upheaval. Soldiers and evacuees come to billet. Wives of men gone to the wars are 'no better than they ought to be'. Wars bring out a febrile vindictiveness as well as heroism. All seems in flux. In this, gossip plays its role. Children taunted for the sins of their fathers hit back with what they have. In the competition to collect rosehips, or silver paper, or stamps, for the war effort, jealousies boiled over. I was told that I didn't know who my father was.

I thought I did. There he was, sitting at home, with his ARP helmet hanging on the door, and his chips frying on the hob. He might have rolled with the punch, but my mother did not. She would fight for the untruth at the heart of her life. I received vehement denials. Neighbours were visited. Threats were made, and sheepish apologies extracted. That done, my mother had to live with the consequences. Once uttered, the denials had to be sustained. Relatives had to be squared, the first year of my life re-written. Her great fear was stoked, every now and then, by the young blond woman who would drive slowly past the school in the late forties in what I now know to be a Triumph Roadster, quizzing the urchins with a glance. 'They' were back.

There came a point when the pretence no longer took in its sole beneficiary. My father crashed his car. I read the report of his accident avidly. It was not every year that we got into the *Derbyshire Times*. The reports gave his age. He was past sixty and clearly not much older than my mother. I knew no one with a mother who owned to more than forty. To the natural fantasies of childhood came hard evidence. I didn't look like them, had none of my father's skills as a master joiner. I now understood why my mother winced when the local butcher patted me on the head and asked if this were her grandson. But there was no response to hints, or leading questions. I left well alone.

Matters came to a head when I wanted to go to university. The local school was not versed in these things. You did it on your own. The papers came from the distant Oxford college of which none of us had ever heard. We puzzled over them in the flickering light of the Baxendale range. Then there was a flash that came from more than freshly stirred faggots. 'They want my birth certificate,' I said. My mother burst into tears, hunched over the table. My father met this crisis as he had met every one since the Great War; by ignoring it. He looked the other way. I think I mumbled something about how I had always known, that it didn't matter. The heartfelt words I've urged on many since, that adopted people are special children, with a different bond, were not available to me then. The keening went on. Eventually that miracle of suppressed information, the shortened birth certificate, was brought out and sent off.

There have been many times when I have been more frightened, or stricken, in later years. But I have never felt so bereft as I did then, sitting dumbly there while my mother cried for her changeling. Eventually she said, 'You've brought more joy into my life than owt else ever did, and I wanted you to be mine for always.' The unease that university would take me away had intensified this deeper feeling. They had lost me. I would be off on the trail of blood ties, down the valley to the house by the river, from which they had nervously carried me away seventeen years before. I was not best placed to deal with such a nervous collapse. Nowadays, with the passing of the 1965 Children Act and the counselling for both adopters and adoptees, if the latter seek their original birth records, you know what to say, to heal and not to harm.

Perhaps even now the words that should be uttered come too late. So it was with me. I went away to Oxford. In that bright future I had no need of an alternative past. In my last term at Oxford my father died, leaving my mother to linger, disabled in her turn by a stroke. For a year we struggled on, with hospitals and housekeepers, until the day came when the last housekeeper went without warning, and my mother, too frail to travel south to my London flat, inaudible in speech, had to face residence in the local old people's home, overheated now, and tinsel bright, but built by the Poor Law Guardians a century before. To her it was still 'the Union,' a place of ill-omen. As we waited for the ambulance she tugged at me with her usable hand and whispered, a last brave act; 'look in your dad's drawer, and you'll find out about them as once had you.'

Later that day I did. Under his timber catalogues and dog-eared ledgers there was a scruffy envelope, unaddressed. Inside was an ill-typed form from the Petty Sessional Court at Bakewell, urging my parents to Take Notice. And inside that was a long birth certificate, of a kind that I had never seen before, in a name I had never heard. It was a puzzle, even then, to see that this person had the same birthday as mine. But after that moment of revelation my instinct was to chase the departed ambulance. To say to the old lady in it what I should have said before; it is only in the moment of knowing what I was that I can understand what I am – your child. It is twenty years almost to the day since she died. After that I met the family down the valley, found kinship with them, and a wisdom in my original grandfather's house that could have set my folks' worries at rest, had they dared the contact. But they did not. I still wake at times possessed with their fear of loss, and my unwitting failure to assuage it before they were gone.

Mary Whitehouse CBE

Mrs Whitehouse is President of the National Viewers' and Listeners' Association, of which she was a co-founder in 1965 and served as Honorary General Secretary for fifteen years.

At the age of twenty-two she became teacher of Art at Wednesfield School, Wolverhampton until her marriage, after which she left teaching to bring up her family of three sons. From 1960 to 1964 she returned to teaching as Senior Mistress and Senior Art Mistress at Madeley School, Shropshire and in 1964 she co-founded the 'Clean up TV Campaign,' which brought her into the public eye.

Her strongly held beliefs in the upholding of moral standards have rendered Mrs Whitehouse a controversial figure in today's liberal society, but she has never relaxed her views or her efforts and in educational and media circles hers is a voice to be reckoned with and respected.

She was awarded the CBE in 1980.

∞∞∞∞∞∞∞∞∞∞∞∞∞∞∞

It was in the summer of 1953 that I was struck down with a TB infection in my kidneys. My children were then six-, eight- and twelve-years-old and any parent reading this will be able to imagine the difficulties created for the family with mother in bed for fourteen weeks!

A stream of kind friends and relatives worked wonders between them and at the end of that prolonged rest I was pronounced cured. My mother then took me to Tenerife – a very, very different place from what it is today – for a three-week holiday at the end of which I was brown and fit and longing to come home to the family. But not yet. The day before we were due to leave my mother went down with pneumonia and we had to stay another three weeks before she was fit to travel. I used to stand on the edge of the sea and look longingly out across the water!

However, in due course, home we came and I was ready to take up the day to day domestic chores and be a full time Mum again. But it was not ever to be quite the same again. Certainly the TB infection was well and truly dealt with but somehow I did not recover the physical strength which had always enabled me to tackle my job in the house and garden with gusto. For the first time we had to think about some help in the house. We couldn't really afford it, so how about me doing some part-time teaching – though I had not intended to return to work. I rang the Wolverhampton Education Authority to tell them what I had in mind and in the marvellous way these things sometimes work out I had a phone call before the week was out to say that there was a vacancy for a part-time Art teacher in a school just around the corner. I could get the children off to school and be back before they arrived home! And Art was my subject!

So, after fourteen years out of teaching I started again and, as time went on and the children grew up, I increased the hours I spent at school until in 1960 there came this marvellous opportunity to become Senior Mistress and Head of the Art Department at a large Secondary Modern school in Shropshire. It was of course my experience in that role – particularly the Senior Mistress part – which gave rise to all the campaigning work in which I have been involved.

I think it's worth taking a minute to tell the story of that appointment. It had been advertised twelve months previously and I had then been offered the job. But we lived in Wolverhampton and this would have involved me in a return trip of thirty-five miles a day often arriving home after the children. So I turned it down – with some disappointment I may say.

A year later we moved into a village in Shropshire and just after we moved in I casually said to my husband, 'You know, if that job ever became vacant again, I could easily do it from here' and, equally casually, I picked up the evening paper. Difficult perhaps to believe, but there was an advertisement for the same post again! I applied and was appointed though little did I realize just what kind of experience it was going to lead me into!

The year before I was appointed, the Newsome Report on Secondary Education had talked about the importance of sex education and declared that it should be given on the basis of 'chastity before marriage and fidelity within it.' Very little work had been done in this field and before I had been in my job more than a few weeks I found myself one of a group of senior staff in the West Midlands involved in pioneering work in sex education – experience which was central to the whole of our campaign.

Looking back now over all these years I can see the extraordinary pattern of the Lord's hand in everything that happened to me. The illness, its after effects, the return to teaching, my experience in sex education, the way in which in the years since – in spite of human weakness – the Lord has led and strengthened beyond contradiction the certainty that God does have a plan and purpose for all our lives; that all that is required of us is a willingness to place ourselves at his disposal. To trust that he is working and will continue to work not only in the good days but the difficult ones as well.

I find immensely encouraging the clause in the new Education Act which calls upon teachers to give sex education based not upon the 'free for all' philosophy which has characterized so much of this teaching – in the media as well as in some of the schools – during the last two and a half decades but within the context of morality and family life. It also reinforces my belief that the Lord does have all things in His hands and will work them out in His own time and in His way, not ours!